"There is vibrant interest in historical matters related to the book of Kings, and anyone seeking an outline of key questions in the current debate will welcome this timely study, as the authors engage with a broad number of secondary sources and provide a clear and succinct contribution to the present debate."

—KEITH BODNER,
professor of religious studies, Crandall University

"David Schreiner and Kyle Greenwood illuminate the thorny historical issues surrounding the Omride dynasty in Northern Israel. The accounts of Omri, Ahab, Ahaziah and Joram recorded in 1 and 2 Kings are perilous to navigate for any interpreter. Commentators have long questioned the internal consistency of the accounts, their redactional complexity, and how they relate to the ancient records left by other nations. This work proposes salient solutions. Schreiner and Greenwood devote equal attention to the various historical voices as to the literary forces that shape the Biblical accounts. And they do this with a keen eye to how the genre of historiography functions as part of Scripture. This study is essential reading for any student of the period."

—NATHAN LOVELL,
director of research, George Whitefield College, Cape Town

"Greenwood and Schreiner deftly combine historical reconstruction with ancient historiography in this compelling examination of the Omride wars. Critically engaging pertinent texts and artifacts, the authors enhance understanding of the poetics of the biblical critique of the Omride dynasty. Challenging the war accounts as late interpolations, this thoughtful and informed volume is valuable for its methodological integration of historical and historiographical perspectives. A welcome read!"

—LISSA M. WRAY BEAL,
professor of Old Testament, Providence Theological Seminary

"The authors provide a thorough review of the primary source data for analyzing and interpreting these political events of the ninth century, that were critical to the kingdoms of Judah and Israel as well as to Damascus. Refusing to accept an analysis that rejects the value of either the biblical or extrabiblical textual sources, the result is a satisfying probe into the crux issues of this history as well as reasonable directions for possible solutions and for further research. Every student of this period and every serious teacher of the relevant biblical texts will want to consult this valuable asset."

—RICHARD S. HESS,
distinguished professor of Old Testament, Denver Seminary

T0338982

"In their examination, Greenwood and Schreiner carefully engage with ancient sources as well as contemporary scholarship. In doing so, the authors not only give an insightful explanation of the background and context for this material but also provide a fresh methodology for anyone interested in Israel's history."

—DAVID T. LAMB,
MacRae Professor of Old Testament
and dean of the faculty, Missio Seminary;
author of God Behaving Badly and Prostitutes and Polygamists

"With literary sensitivity and deeply informed awareness of the context, Greenwood and Schreiner demonstrate the possibilities of an informed and careful way of critically integrating the biblical material with other sources. Their work thus not only sheds light on the fall of the Omride dynasty in Israel, it also provides promising pathways for the future integration of this material."

—DAVID G. FIRTH,
tutor in Old Testament, Trinity College Bristol

"In this exciting and well-written book, Kyle Greenwood and David Schreiner offer a fascinating study of the Omride wars thanks to their vast knowledge of biblical exegesis, extrabiblical sources, and archaeological excavations. But they do more than that: they also offer a behind-the-scenes look at the historical method. I admire the way they get to the heart of the questions, lay out the scholarly debates with clarity, and put forward their own interpretation based on arguments that illustrate their careful approach. The result is both an excellent introduction to the issues that historians face when they try to reconstruct the history of ancient Israel, and a manifesto for a balanced and lucid historiographical method."

—MATTHIEU RICHELLE,
professeur d'exégèse de l'Ancien Testament,
Université Catholique de Louvain

AHAB'S HOUSE OF HORRORS

A Historiographic Study of the Military Campaigns of the House of Omri

See also these titles from the
Lexham Geographic Commentary Series,
edited by Barry J. Beitzel

Lexham Geographic Commentary on the Gospels

Lexham Geographic Commentary on Acts through Revelation

*Lexham Geographic Commentary on
the Pentateuch (forthcoming)*

*Lexham Geographic Commentary on the
Historical Books, vols. 1 & 2 (forthcoming)*

*Lexham Geographic Commentary on
Poetry and Prophecy (forthcoming)*

For updates on this series, visit
LexhamPress.com/Geographic-Commentary

AHAB'S HOUSE OF HORRORS

A Historiographic Study of the Military Campaigns of the House of Omri

Studies in Biblical Archaeology, Geography, and History

KYLE R. GREENWOOD AND
DAVID B. SCHREINER

Series Editor: Barry J. Beitzel

LEXHAM PRESS

Ahab's House of Horrors: A Historiographic Study of the Military Campaigns of the House of Omri
Studies in Biblical Archaeology, Geography, and History

Copyright 2023 Kyle R. Greenwood and David B. Schreiner

Lexham Press, 1313 Commercial St., Bellingham, WA 98225
LexhamPress.com

Unless otherwise noted, Scripture quotations are the authors' own translation.

Print ISBN 9781683596486
Digital ISBN 9781683596493
Library of Congress Control Number 2022948724

Series Editor: Barry J. Beitzel
Lexham Editorial: Douglas Mangum, Neal Huddleston, Amy Balogh, Danielle Burlaga, Mandi Newell, Abigail Stocker
Cover Design: Brittany Schrock
Typesetting: ProjectLuz.com

With gratitude to
Bill Arnold and Lawson Stone:
scholars, mentors, friends

CONTENTS

ILLUSTRATIONS

FIGURES

MAPS

TABLES

PREFACE

At the 2017 annual meeting of the Society of Biblical Literature and the Institute for Biblical Research in Boston, MA, we presented separate papers related to 1 Kings.[1] Incidentally, we had both cut our academic teeth at Asbury Theological Seminary in the late '90s (Kyle) and early 2000s (David), both having studied under the tutelage of Bill Arnold and Lawson Stone, among others. These common bonds led to subsequent discussions about our shared interest in Israel's historical record, especially with how it comports to the historical records of their neighbors. Rather than continuing these pursuits in different directions, we decided to join forces and collaborate.

For most of the first several hundred years of Israel's history there is little extrabiblical textual evidence available for comparison. With the turn of the ninth century BC, however, numerous texts emerged that have direct bearing on the biblical events, particularly with reference to the Omride dynasty. Some of these texts identify biblical characters in contexts that coincide, at least in principle, with the Bible's historical accounting. Intriguingly, while the biblical history paints Jehoshaphat in a generally positive light and the Omride family in an overtly negative light, the extrabiblical evidence tells another

---

1. Kyle R. Greenwood, "Anonymous Biblical Kings in Light of the Assyrian and Babylonian Chronicles"; David B. Schreiner, "'Now Rehoboam Son of Solomon Reigned in Judah': Pondering the Semantic and Structural Significance of 1 Kings 14:21."

story, with the Omrides actively building architectural structures, an impressive military, and an efficient government.[2] For us, then, the Omride wars as recounted in 1 Kings 20 and 22, and 2 Kings 3 provide an obvious point of intersection to investigate the phenomenon of biblical historiography.

In many respects, our investigation into the Omride wars yields unsurprising findings, at least from our perspective. As is the case with most projects, we are also delighted to have also uncovered some unexpected results that have helped frame our thesis. We hope that this project will meaningfully contribute to the ongoing discussion of biblical historiography in general, and the history of the Omride family specifically.

---

2. Brad E. Kelle and Brent A. Strawn, "History of Israel 5: Assyrian Period," in *Dictionary of the Old Testament: Historical Books*, ed. Bill T. Arnold and H. G. M. Williamson (Downers Grove, IL: IVP Academic, 2005), 458–78, esp. 463.

ACKNOWLEDGMENTS

From Kyle and David: We are indebted to the Old Testament department faculty of Asbury Theological Seminary who honed our exegetical skills, challenged us to think critically on issues of biblical historiography, and encouraged us in our academic pursuits. The lessons we learned from our formal training continue to influence our scholarship. In addition, we extend a big thank-you to Nathan Lovell, who was willing to read through our manuscript and offer perceptive critiques and insights. We are especially grateful for Barry Beitzel, Doug Mangum, Amy Balogh, and Lexham Press for their willingness to publish our manuscript in the series Studies in Biblical Archaeology, Geography, and History. Doug has been supportive of our project and willing to deal with our copious questions as we prepared the manuscript.

From Kyle: Over a decade ago, Bill Arnold and Rick Hess invited me to contribute to *Ancient Israel's History: An Introduction to Issues and Sources*, in which I wrote the chapter dealing with late tenth- and ninth-century issues.[1] I've been pondering the perplexities of the Omride family ever since, especially with respect to the historical

---

1. Kyle R. Greenwood, "Late Tenth- and Ninth-Century Issues: Ahab Underplayed? Jehoshaphat Overplayed?," in *Ancient Israel's History: An Introduction to Issues and Sources*, ed. Bill T. Arnold and Richard S. Hess (Grand Rapids: Baker Academic, 2014), 286–318.

complications of the biblical text when compared and contrasted with extrabiblical sources. I even considered authoring my own book on the Omride wars, but another writing project had me preoccupied for the foreseeable future, shelving this project indefinitely. It received new life, though, when David and I began our discussions in 2017. With David stepping in doing much of the most time-consuming work, the project was revived. It has been my pleasure to work alongside David and the book is much better than if I had written it solo.

I wish to thank my friends and co-laborers at Development Associates International for encouraging me to stay connected to the world of academia. I wish to express my thanks to the faculties of Denver Seminary and Fuller Theological Seminary for their continued support in my role as an affiliated faculty member. Finally, I want to thank Karen and our three adult children who inspire me with their work ethic, critical thinking, pursuit of adventure, and dedication to justice.

From David: The Omride dynasty has always been a topic of interest for me. As the son of a United Methodist minister, I grew up in church. Consequently, the accounts of Scripture became familiar very early in my upbringing. Because I have always liked history, these and the other stories of the historical books became some of my favorites. With exposure to issues of archaeology and ancient Near Eastern history during my formal education, my interest in them and questions about them were ratcheted up several notches. How can the Omride family be so villainized and yet be remembered outside the pages of Scripture so positively? What does this tell us about the nature of biblical history writing and the dynamics of Scripture in general? Therefore, I am grateful to Kyle for allowing me to come alongside him and help him flesh out some ideas regarding this family and the manner in which they are presented in the pages of Scripture.

I would be remiss not to extend my thanks to others as well, especially all my professors at Asbury Theological Seminary who challenged me to think critically on issues of biblical historiography.

Thanks is also extended to Wesley Biblical Seminary for allowing me to write this manuscript as the world was affected by COVID-19. Most importantly, I thank my family. To my parents who introduced me to the Bible. To my dad who instilled within me a love for Scripture and a foundation to engage it properly. To my brothers who always graciously show an interest in my chosen vocation, even though I know they are rolling their eyes internally. To my daughters, Maddie, Bailey, and Lily, for their ability to ask the questions that seem to matter most: "Daddy, how does this matter to our Sunday School classes?" To my lovely wife Ginny. Her willingness to put up with my weird interests and to selflessly entertain the kids so I can edit one more page or put one more thought on paper is a Godsend. I am a better man because of her.

I hope that this project shows a commitment to understanding the function and message of Scripture on the terms with which it was originally written.

ABBREVIATIONS

AB	Anchor Bible
ABD	*Anchor Bible Dictionary*. Edited by David Noel Freedman. 6 vols. New York: Doubleday, 1992
ABS	Archaeology and Biblical Studies
ANET	*Ancient Near Eastern Texts Relating to the Old Testament*. Edited by James B. Pritchard. 3rd ed. Princeton: Princeton University Press, 1969
AOTC	Abingdon Old Testament Commentaries
BA	*Biblical Archaeologist*
BAR	*Biblical Archaeology Review*
BASOR	*Bulletin of the American Schools of Oriental Research*
BBR	*Bulletin for Biblical Research*
BN	*Biblische Notizen*
BZAW	Beihefte zur Zeitschrift für die alttestamentliche Wissenschaft
CAD	*The Assyrian Dictionary of the Oriental Institute of the University of Chicago*. 21 vols. Chicago: The Oriental Institute of the University of Chicago, 1956–2010
COS	*The Context of Scripture*. Edited by William Hallo and K. Lawson Younger. 4 vols. Leiden: Brill, 1997–2016

HALOT	*The Hebrew and Aramaic Lexicon of the Old Testament.* Ludwig Koehler, Walter Baumgartner, and Johann J. Stamm. Translated and edited under the supervision of Mervyn E. J. Richardson. 2 vols. Leiden: Brill, 2001
IEJ	*Israel Exploration Journal*
JBL	*Journal of Biblical Literature*
JNES	*Journal of Near Eastern Studies*
JPOS	*Journal of the Palestinian Oriental Society*
JSOT	*Journal for the Study of the Old Testament*
JSOTSup	Journal for the Study of the Old Testament Supplement Series
JTS	*Journal of Theological Studies*
KAI	*Kanaanäische und aramäische Inschriften.* Herbert Donner and Wolfgang Röllig. 2nd ed. Wiesbaden: Harrassowitz, 1966–1969
LHBOTS	The Library of Hebrew Bible/Old Testament Studies
LXX	Septuagint
MT	Masoretic Text
NICOT	New International Commentary on the Old Testament
RB	*Revue Biblique*
RIMA	The Royal Inscriptions of Mesopotamia: Assyrian Periods
SJOT	*Scandinavian Journal of the Old Testament*
TOTC	Tyndale Old Testament Commentaries
VT	*Vetus Testamentum*
WBC	Word Biblical Commentary
ZAW	*Zeitschrift für die alttestamentliche Wissenschaft*

Chapter 1

A PROLOGUE

F irst Kings 12 recounts a strategic moment in the history of ancient Israel. As the chapter begins, Rehoboam meets the delegates of his nation at Shechem for his coronation as the new king of unified Israel. This is a time of transition that also happens to bring a palpable level of vulnerability for the king. Why is he to be coronated at Shechem and not Jerusalem? Shechem was a northern stronghold with deep ties to the politics of the northern region. Thus, the implication is that at the time of his coronation, Rehoboam does not enjoy solid political footing. Of course, these suspicions are quickly verified by the opening verses. The emissaries of the northern tribes approach Rehoboam with a proposal, whereby they ask that their economic burdens be lightened. If their request is granted, then they will fall in line with his reign (1 Kgs 12:4). Thus, it is clear that the policies of his father Solomon had exacerbated rifts between the tribes of Israel.

As the chapter unfolds, the situation takes a turn for the worst. Rehoboam displays not only a lack of wisdom, but he also resigns himself to his insecurities when he accepts the advice of his unproven and privileged counselors. The result? The northern tribes break away, declaring that they no longer will have anything to do with David's line and the capital in Jerusalem (1 Kgs 12:16). What was once a unified nation became two separate nations until 722 BC when the northern kingdom was overrun by the Neo-Assyrian Empire. But more to the point, the era of the divided monarchy was characterized by inconsistent relationships between the two kingdoms. Sometimes Judah and Israel worked together for common goals and the betterment of their societies and cultures. Other times, they were at each other's throats. In fact, hostility defined the early years of the divided monarchy. First Kings 14 through 16 documents continual skirmishes and conflicts between Judah and Israel, even stating that war defined their relationship from the reigns of Rehoboam through Asa in the south, and Jeroboam through Elah in the north (1 Kgs 15:6, 32). Thus, a picture is painted of a geopolitical mess where alliances were broken, betrayals incited, and self-preservation was the norm.

Eventually, the Israelite general Omri asserted himself on the scene. According to 1 Kings 16:15–16, a large group of influential people within Israelite society facilitated the crowning of Omri in rejection of the coup d'état by Zimri, one of Elah's two chariotry commanders (1 Kgs 16:8–10). In turn, Omri marshalled his troops and quickly dispatched the usurper. However, this course of action produced another obstacle for Omri. Tibni, another claimant to the throne, was recognized by some within Israel in the wake of Zimri's assassination (1 Kgs 16:21). In other words, Omri's dispatching of Zimri produced more problems, forcing him to deal with a rival claim to the throne. Nevertheless, Tibni's claim did not last long as the supporters of Omri overwhelmed the supporters of Tibni (1 Kgs 16:22), and Omri quickly solidified his claim to the Israelite throne. Omri then purchased the region around Samaria from a man named Shemer in order to build a new capital, symbolizing a new era of Israelite history. But to take it a step further, this new capital also provided a newfound stability in the region, for such infrastructure investments were impossible in the years leading up to Omri's inauguration. Similar to Solomon's heavy-handed policies, Omri's violence provided a new phase of cultural development for Israel (see 1 Kgs 3–10).

Omri initiated a relatively short-lived dynasty that functioned effectively during the middle portion of the ninth century BC. Although—as we will discuss throughout this study—there are some very sticky chronological difficulties with demarcating the length of their reigns precisely.

TABLE 1: The Omride dynasty

Omri	(876–69 BC)
↓	
Ahab	(869–50 BC)
↓	
Ahaziah	(850–49 BC)
↓	
J(eh)oram[1]	(849–42 BC)

In spite of this apparent success, the book of Kings quickly notes that Omri "did evil in the eyes of Yahweh" by persisting in the sins of Jeroboam I. In fact, Omri did more evil "than all who were before him" (1 Kgs 16:25–26). Moreover, the reader does not have to progress much further to realize that Omri's family, particularly his son Ahab, appeared at the center of much national controversy. Immediately after Ahab's succession to the throne, the reader is informed of Ahab's syncretism, diplomatic marriage to the Sidonian princess Jezebel, and his collusion in the formal establishment of Baalism (1 Kgs 16:29–32). And if that was not enough, Ahab surpassed his father's apostasy

---

1. The spelling of J(eh)oram warrants a brief comment at the onset of this study. In the biblical witness, there are two spellings, and each may be linked to specific dialectical tendencies. The Israelite dialect, the Hebrew spoken in the northern kingdom, likely spelled the name as יוֹרָם (yôrām). In Judah, the name was likely spelled יְהוֹרָם (yəhôrām). While some suppose that these dialectical differences should inform the conversation regarding sources and chronology, others assert that the spelling in Kings is arbitrary (for an example, see John Strange, "Joram, King of Israel and Judah," VT 25.2 [1975]: 192 n. 7). As much as possible we seek to honor this ongoing debate by spelling the name as J(eh)oram. However, when we quote or directly invoke other scholars, their spelling is retained.

with flying colors. According to 1 Kings 16:33, "Ahab continued to do things to incite Yahweh, God of Israel, to anger, more than all the kings of Israel who were before him." The Omride dynasty is probably most famous for their public hostility toward Yahweh's prophets (see 1 Kgs 18).

Consequently, the Old Testament quickly vilifies the Omride dynasty. Yet this focused presentation creates a significant difficulty vis-à-vis the extrabiblical testimony of the dynasty. Several inscriptions and archaeological evidence suggest that the Omrides' effect on the region was positive.[2] For example, the Kurkh Monolith illustrates Ahab's resourcefulness and capabilities with the sizable military force marshalled for the Syro-Palestinian coalition against the Assyrians at Qarqar (see chapter 2). The Moabite Stone testifies to Omride imperialism and geopolitical influence in the region (see chapter 6), and the Tel Dan Stele celebrates the defeat of the dynasty in a way that testifies to its regional dominance (see chapter 2). Archaeologically speaking, the architecture of Samaria displays undeniable marks of cultural sophistication. Whether in monumental architecture or small finds, both the quality of the material finds and the construction itself suggests a society that had resources, ambition, and a will to develop a cultural brand. In addition, locations through the region (e.g., Jezreel) display evidence of development and cultural continuity with Samaria.

For some, the net result of these divergent sources produces a manageable tension. For others, it produces a historical barrier that potentially destabilizes the veracity of the Old Testament. In many cases, allegiance must be declared. Either one must exclusively accept the biblical representation of the dynasty as the testimony that matters, effectively questioning any positive influence the dynasty had on the region, or one must exclusively accept the extrabiblical testimony, thereby calling into question the viability and usefulness of the

---

2. Greenwood, "Late Tenth- and Ninth-Century Issues," 292–301; David B. Schreiner, "Omride Dynasty," in *The Lexham Bible Dictionary*, ed. John D. Barry (Bellingham, WA: Lexham Press, 2016), digital.

Old Testament. Admittedly, the stakes are high, for the latter scenario has proven to have lasting implications within certain Christian academic traditions. If the biblical presentation of the Omride dynasty is so slanted—beyond the point that it can be trusted to contain any historical value—then what does it have to say about other historical claims in the Old Testament? Are all the claims in the Old Testament so ideologically slanted that they are beyond historical usefulness?

We believe that such an "either/or" scenario is problematic. For starters, such a black-and-white position harkens back to the debates between the so-called "minimalists" and "maximalists." These debates were widespread toward the end of the twentieth century and into the twenty-first century dividing scholars who believe there is historical value in the Old Testament against those who do not. And as you might expect, caricaturization soon defined the interaction. Such caricaturization produces strawmen in order to expose perceived fallacies. This, in turn, produced a centrist position that was so diffuse that essentially anyone could lay claim to that point on the academic spectrum. So, as everyone claimed a centrist position, it quickly became meaningless.

The unintended consequence of the minimalist-maximalist debate—namely, the over-saturation of the centrist position—nevertheless sheds light on the philosophical problems of the "either/or" scenario. To put it bluntly, such a scenario is just not viable. The historical difficulties associated with the Omride dynasty, which are mirrored throughout the Old Testament, cannot be navigated with a simplistic declaration of allegiance to a particular pool of data, like a fan that myopically roots for their favorite team. Determining whether one is partial to "Team Bible" against all other contenders will neither solve nor alleviate the difficulties. And the same can be said about allegiance to "Team Archaeology" or "Team Assyrian Inscriptions." As will become clear in this study, the dynamics of historical reconstruction and ancient history writing are too nuanced. One *must* move beyond the black and white and embrace the gray.

Consequently, this study seeks to embrace the gray by engaging the complex dynamics of ancient history writing and the historical difficulties of the Omride dynasty. Yet the historical difficulties of the Omrides is a well-trodden trail. In order to avoid getting lost in the crowd, we have chosen to focus on a single element of the problem that is ripe for further nuance: the Omride wars of 1 Kings 20, 22, and 2 Kings 3. However, discussing the Omride wars is not completely uncharted territory. Among some very influential voices, these chapters are understood to be accounts from a later period of Israel's history, only to have been transposed onto a ninth-century-BC context because a Judean author wanted to intensify an anti-Omride polemic. In this view, these military accounts are more vehicles of propaganda, rather than vehicles of historical reality. However, others argue that it is unnecessary to see these war accounts as incompatible within the larger Omride context. We agree with the latter camp, particularly since the data points marshalled in support of a complicated editorial program can be interpreted differently. Such nuance requires an awareness of the canons of ancient history writing synthesized with the testimony of the extrabiblical witnesses that speak to the exploits of this dynasty. Thus, the proper posture in navigating the historical difficulty of the Omrides is not an "either/or" proposition, as if either the biblical or non-biblical testimony should be valued above all others. Instead, an intelligent synthesis of all the applicable witnesses is required.

Chapter 2 opens our argument by engaging the end of the Omride dynasty through the biblical and Aramaic witnesses, namely 2 Kings 9–10 and the Tel Dan Stele. While the stele is usually employed regarding the historicity of David and the united monarchy, we invoke it to demonstrate our governing method, though it has something to say about the Omride dynasty as well. Ultimately, we show what an intelligent synthesis between biblical and extrabiblical testimonies looks like.

Chapter 3 opens with Israel's battle with Aram at Samaria (1 Kgs 20:1–22). The chapter also addresses the lengthy historical relationship between these powers, the difficulty surrounding the identity of the king of Aram, and the anonymity of Israel's kings throughout 1 Kings 20, 22, and 2 Kings 3. Many of the conclusions in this chapter are foundational to our study.

Chapter 4 discusses Israel's war with Aram at Aphek and features Ahab's second encounter with Ben-Hadad in 1 Kings 20:23–34. The chapter also engages the identification of Israel's army as "two little flocks of goats." This traditional translation is evaluated, and an alternative understanding is offered that mitigates the perceived friction between the biblical account and certain Assyrian records.

Chapter 5 focuses on the battle of Ramoth-Gilead as outlined in 1 Kings 22:1–40. The chapter deals with the location of Ramoth-Gilead, the dynamics of the battle there, and the problematic sequence of dynastic succession in the Omride family.

Chapter 6 discusses Israel's war with Moab. In particular, the biblical witness is compared with Mesha's inscription, which has been pitted as contradictory to 2 Kings 3. We argue that the historical witnesses can be synthesized and, like the witness of the Tel Dan Stele with 2 Kings 9–10, both the biblical and Moabite sources testify to a complicated socio-political situation.

The closing chapter offers some final thoughts and concludes the argument that has been developing through the previous chapters. In particular, we focus on 1 Kings 20, 22, and 2 Kings 3 and propose that the chapters constitute a sustained and systematic critique of Omride military policy. We propose that the biblical presentation utilizes a convention of general anonymity to relegate personalities under institutions and to focus upon methods of operation. Specifically, the biblical presentation targets the Omride tendency to value political opportunity at the expense of Deuteronomic concerns. Moreover, this defiant policy secured Ahab's judgment, thereby situating the events of 1 Kings 20 and 22 on a historical continuum that sees the death of Omri and J(eh)oram's decisive defeat in Moab.

Chapter 2

TEL DAN, 2 KINGS 9–10, AND
THE HISTORICAL TENSION:
A STUDY IN METHOD

I n 1993 and 1995 Avraham Biran and Joseph Naveh published their readings of a fragmented Aramaic inscription excavated from various places throughout a particular Iron Age stratum at Tel Dan.[1] The Tel Dan Stele consists of three fragments of various sizes and shapes, each of which was found in secondary usage. What Biran and Naveh translated rocked the landscape of Old Testament studies. They confidently proclaimed that the phrase "House of David" was inscribed on the surface of Fragment A, thus constituting extrabiblical attestation of the dynasty's founder. This was significant as it serendipitously came in the wake of influential histories on ancient Israel that openly questioned widely and long-held historical assumptions regarding the historicity of King David and the united monarchy.[2]

---

1. Avraham Biran and Joseph Naveh, "An Aramaic Stele Fragment from Tel Dan," *IEJ* 43.2–3 (1993): 81–98; Biran and Naveh, "The Tel Dan Inscription: A New Fragment," *IEJ* 45.1 (1995): 1–18.

2. One particularly influential group was the so-called Copenhagen School, so named due to the affiliation of two of its most prominent figures with the University of Copenhagen, Niels

FIGURE 1: **The Tel Dan Stele**

Biran and Naveh's translation of the Tel Dan Stele is as follows:

[...] and cut [...]

[...] my father went up [against him when] he fought at [...]

And my father lay down, he went to his [ancestors]

Peter Lemche and Thomas L. Thompson. Two scholars from the University of Sheffield joined this school of thought—Philip R. Davies and Keith W. Whitelam (see Niels Peter Lemche, *Ancient Israel: A New History of Israelite History*, The Biblical Seminar 5 [Sheffield: JSOT Press, 1988]; Philip R. Davies, *In Search of "Ancient Israel*," JSOTSup 148 [Sheffield: JSOT Press, 1992]; Thomas L. Thompson, *Early History of the Israelite People*, Studies in the History of the Ancient Near East 4 [Leiden: Brill, 1992]; Whitelam, *The Invention of Ancient Israel: The Silencing of Palestinian History* [London: Routledge, 1996]).

And the king of I[s--]
rael entered previously in my father's land. [And] Hadad made me king.
And Hadad went in front of me, [and] I departed from [the] seven [...]
s of my kingdom, and I slew [seve]nty kin[gs], who harnessed thou[sands of char--]
riots and thousands of horsemen (or: horses). [I killed Jeho]ram son of [Ahab]
king of Israel, and [I] killed [Ahaz]iahu son of [Jehoram kin--]
g of the House of David. And I set [their towns into ruins and turned]
their land into [desolation ...]

other [...   and Jehu ru--]
led over Is[rael ...   and I laid]
siege upon [...][3]

Proponents of the Bible's historicity trumpeted the Tel Dan Stele
fragments as a type of magic bullet, presuming it would silence all
the skeptics. However, the skeptics doubled down, and in many cases
sought to chip away at Biran and Naveh's argument. For instance,
Ernst Knauf, D. de Pury, and Thomas Römer maintained that reading "House of David" created an unacceptable awkwardness vis-à-vis
the other clauses and reconstructed words in the immediate context.[4]
Niels Peter Lemche and Thomas L. Thompson proposed that the
consonants *bytdwd* (ביתדוד) were more closely analogous to a place
name, like Bethel, versus a dynastic title.[5] Then there was the lack
of a word divider between "house" and "David." For many, this was
problematic, particularly since word dividers are used throughout the
inscription. In some cases, the integrity of the excavation was even
called into question. In one instance, Lemche accused the excavators
of faking photographs, and in another, more peculiar instance, Russel

---

3. Biran and Naveh, "A New Fragment," 13.

4. Ernst Axel Knauf, D. de Pury, and Thomas Römer, "*Baytdawid ou *Baytdod? Une
relecture de la nouvelle inscription de Tel Dan," *BN* 72 (1994): 65–66.

5. Niels Lemche and Thomas L. Thompson, "Did Biran Kill David? The Bible in Light of
Archaeology," *JSOT* 64 (1994): 9.

Gmirkin suggested that the inscription was added after the stele was destroyed.[6] Consequently, in just a few short years after the initial publications of the Tel Dan Stele, certain trajectories for the debate were set. During the next two decades, epigraphists, historians, and biblical scholars waded through the discussions, nuanced their arguments, bolstered conclusions, and dismissed tenuous and dubious claims. Ultimately, this discussion has overwhelmingly accepted the legitimacy of the inscription, the presence of the phrase "the House of David," and the phrase's reference to a longstanding Judean dynasty founded by a royal figure named David.[7] This discussion has also demonstrated the importance of the Tel Dan Stele for understanding the dynamics of Israelite historiography.

The critical issue that proceeds from the fierce debates surrounding the Tel Dan Stele is precisely who ended the Omride dynasty.[8] Although lines 7–8 are fragmentary, many scholars accept the reconstruction that J(eh)oram of Israel and Ahaziah of Judah are mentioned.[9] Thus, the author of the stele, who is generally identified as the Aramean Hazael of Damascus, is claiming to have defeated and killed them both. Initially such a claim appears to go against the biblical account, in which Jehu becomes the divinely anointed assassin of the Omrides (2 Kgs 9). According to the biblical account, he systematically hunts down and slaughters the remnants of the family, including Jezebel. In the midst of this, Jehu meets J(eh)oram and

---

6. Hershel Shanks, ed., "Biblical Minimalists Meet Their Challengers Face to Face," *BAR* 23.4 (1997): 26–42, 66; Russel Gmirkin, "Tool Slippage and the Tel Dan Inscription," *SJOT* 16 (2002): 293–302.

7. For details, see Hallvard Hagelia, *The Dan Debate: The Tel Dan Inscription in Recent Research*, Recent Research in Biblical Studies 4 (Sheffield: Sheffield Phoenix Press, 2009).

8. See David B. Schreiner, *Pondering the Spade: Discussing Important Convergences between Archaeology and Old Testament Studies* (Eugene, OR: Wipf and Stock, 2019), 100–102.

9. To be clear there are several proposed reconstructions for these lines. For a chart that summarizes the possibilities, see K. Lawson Younger Jr., "'Hazael, Son of a Nobody': Some Reflections in Light of Recent Study," in *Writing and Ancient Near Eastern Study: Papers in Honour of Alan R. Millard*, LHBOTS 426, ed. Piotr Bienkowski, Christopher Mee, and Elizabeth Slater (New York: T&T Clark, 2005), 251–52.

Ahaziah on the battlefield. But as J(eh)oram flees, Jehu shoots him dead. Consequently, such a blatant tension has inspired certain unimpeachable statements: e.g., "Obviously, if Hazael killed Jehoram and Ahaziah, the biblical story of how Jehu killed them must be historically incorrect."[10] So who has the rightful claim of putting an end to the Omride dynasty? And if the Old Testament is incorrect, what does this reveal about the Old Testament's historiographic method? Or is a more nuanced reading possible?

2.1 ATTEMPTS TO EXPLAIN THE TENSION

There have been several attempts to clarify this historical difficulty, and each falls into one of three categories. First, some argue that no real conflict exists. For example, Jan-Wim Wesselius proposed that Jehu was the author of the stele, removing the tension altogether.[11] Wesselius emphasizes that the biblical claim that Jehu killed off the Omride dynasty cannot be dismissed out of hand, and it is preferable to first disprove the main witness before moving to alternative theories. Thus, Wesselius's argument is largely a rebuttal that a Jehu-origin is dubious.

Wesselius begins his argument by exploring the legitimacy of an Aramaic inscription by an Israelite if Jehu was either a vassal or a supporter of Hazael's coup, a perspective that other scholars accept. Because Jehu demonstrated an accepting posture early in his reign (2 Kgs 10:18), it is not beyond reason for Jehu to initially praise Hadad for his ascension, which is what the Tel Dan Stele does. It is also well within the characteristics of royal literature in the ancient Near East to declare divine support in committing regicide. Finally, referring to an Aramean king as his "father" is expected in contexts where one party (i.e., Jehu) is subservient to the other (the Aramean king).

---

10. J. Maxwell Miller and John H. Hayes, *A History of Ancient Israel and Judah*, 2nd ed. (Louisville: Westminster John Knox, 2006), 325.

11. Jan-Wim Wesselius, "The First Royal Inscription from Ancient Israel: The Tel Dan Inscription Reconsidered," *SJOT* 13.2 (1999): 163–86.

Wesselius was criticized by Bob Becking and then again by George Athas.[12] However, in 2001, before Athas's criticisms, Wesselius went on record saying that he was even more convinced in the wake of Becking's response.[13] But in the end, it is difficult to accept Wesselius's ideas. While he rightly champions not dismissing the biblical account out-of-hand, and while there are many who envision a political arrangement between Jehu and Hazael, there are too many contingencies for this scenario to play out. Wesselius's ideas are plausible, but not probable.

Second, others argue that either the Tel Dan Stele or the biblical account is to be preferred in any historical reconstruction. On the one hand, Nadav Na'aman reasons that the stele is to be the "point of departure for the historical discussion."[14] According to Na'aman, the lengthy history of composition and literary development associated with the biblical narrative "blurs" the historical memory while the stele represents a contemporary account of the events.[15] Moreover, Na'aman believes that featuring an event in which the author (Hazael) did not take part strains credulity. Ingo Kottsieper also believes that the stele represents the more reliable voice in the matter. According to Kottsieper, the Tel Dan Stele publicly justified Aramean movements against Israel, which was necessary as there was an alliance between Jehu and Hazael.[16]

---

12. George Athas, *The Tel Dan Inscription: A Reappraisal and a New Introduction*, LHBOTS 360 (New York: T&T Clark, 2006), 257; Bob Becking, "Did Jehu Write the Tel Dan Inscription?" *SJOT* 13 (1999): 187–201.

13. Jan-Wim Wesselius, "The Road to Jezreel: Primary History and the Tel Dan Inscription," *SJOT* 15 (2001): 83–103.

14. Nadav Na'aman, "Three Notes on the Aramaic Inscription from Tel Dan," *IEJ* 50 (2000): 103.

15. Na'aman, "Three Notes," 103.

16. See Ingo Kottsieper, "The Tel Dan Inscription (KAI 310) and the Political Relations Between Aram-Damascus and Israel in the First Half of the First Millennium BC," in *Ahab Agonistes: The Rise and Fall of the Omri Dynasty*, ed. Lester Grabbe (New York: T&T Clark, 2007), 104–34. Kottsieper also points out that Jehu stayed in Ramoth-Gilead after the Aramean victory, suggesting an alliance. However, at some point, said alliance was fractured, resulting in the Aramean hostilities referenced in the stele.

On the other hand, André Lemaire believes the biblical witness to be more contemporary than the Aramaic stele and therefore to be preferred.[17] According to Lemaire, the Tel Dan Stele is fundamentally propagandistic and apologetic. It seeks to establish Hazael's legitimacy to the throne. He was, however, a usurper and therefore required divine support to be viewed as a legitimate king. The Tel Dan Stele offers that support. It is therefore reasonable to expect a rival explanation for the event.

The ideas of Lemaire and Na'aman demonstrate the tenuousness of the debate. One can make a reasonable argument for the superiority of either the biblical account or the Tel Dan Stele. Moreover, that argument is largely contingent on one's suppositions about the literary development of the historical books. If their composition was largely an Iron Age phenomenon (e.g., Lemaire), then preferring the biblical account is reasonable. However, if one believes that their development was a later phenomenon (e.g., Na'aman), then the Tel Dan Stele is the preferred source, as it was composed closer to the actual event.

Third, still others argue that both texts preserve important historical realities, and that both need to be critically and carefully read. For example, William Schniedewind argued that both the Tel Dan Stele and the biblical account bear witness to a historical alliance between Jehu and Hazael.[18] Thus, the Tel Dan Stele and the biblical account both offer legitimate, but different, perspectives of the same event. According to Schniedewind, Jehu's killing of the remnants of the Omride dynasty effectively nullified an existing treaty between Israel and Phoenicia.[19] Therefore, in the wake of that political

---

17. André Lemaire, "The Tel Dan Stele as a Piece of Royal Historiography," *JSOT* 81 (1998): 10–11.

18. William M. Schniedewind, "Tel Dan Stela: New Light on Aramaic and Jehu's Revolt," *BASOR* 302 (1996): 75–90.

19. Schniedewind, "Tel Dan Stela," 83. Schniedewind's use of the term Phoenicia in describing such an alliance appears too imprecise. Hélène Sader has recently reiterated that the term describes a series of four territories connected by an observable cultural footprint. In fact, she states that these territories around Arvad, Byblos, Sidon, and Tyre "never united to form a unified polity, and there is no evidence that their inhabitants ever identified themselves as belonging to one people or one nation" (Sader, *The History and Archaeology of Phoenicia*, ABS 25

collapse, Jehu was forced to look elsewhere for political support. Hazael then stepped into that void, which in turn emboldened Jehu to step away from Ramoth-Gilead and dispatch J(eh)oram and Ahaziah. Schniedewind argues that Jehu was a vassal of Hazael, and, as the suzerain, Hazael can claim that he "killed" J(eh)oram and Ahaziah on the stele. While Schniedewind's reconstruction is possible, it remains unverified. Although he offers support for his reconstruction in the curious connection between Jehu, Hazael, and certain prophets (1 Kgs 19:15–18), his reconstruction struggles with (1) painting a convincing picture of Jehu's vassalship under Hazael, and with (2) imagining a scenario by which Jehu removes himself from the battlefield at Ramoth-Gilead to utilize a newly enacted treaty.

Some suggest that the verb *qtl (קתל) in the Tel Dan Stele is critical to understanding any potential collaboration between sources. According to Shigeo Yamada, this root does not necessarily refer to "killing," as is often proposed. Rather, it suggests something more general, such as "defeat" or "striking."[20] Thus, the inscription may be saying that J(eh)oram and Ahaziah "were defeated" or "struck down." Such a proposal is intriguing, as the lack of explicit agency allows the message of the stele to stand beside the biblical account without any threat of historical conflict. Yamada's proposal has struggled to gain acceptance. For example, Kottsieper does not find it convincing, and Na'aman points out that "this interpretation does not concord with the usual meaning of the verb *qtl in Aramaic texts."[21]

In contrast, Anson Rainey reads a passive sense in *qtl.[22] He does so by proposing two different orthographic and grammatical scenarios, both of which accomplish the same purpose. First, he entertains

[Atlanta: SBL Press, 2019], 313). Therefore, if Schniedewind's premise is on target, the political fallout would likely be with Sidon only.

20. Shigeo Yamada, "Aram Israel Relations as Reflected in the Aramaic Inscription from Tel Dan," *Ugarit-Forschungen* 27 (1995): 619–20.

21. Kottsieper, "Tel Dan Inscription," 125 n. 86; Na'aman, "Three Notes," 101.

22. Anson Rainey and R. Steven Notley, *The Sacred Bridge: Carta's Atlas of the Biblical World* (Jerusalem: Carta, 2006), 212–13.

the possibility of an internal *matres lectionis* as the theme vowel in a reconstructed *qətīl* form, based on the Tel Fekheriyeh inscription as precedence. However, he admits that it was probably written without the internal *matres lectionis*. Second, Rainey proposes reading **qtl* in lines 7 and 8 as a third person common plural form as opposed to a first person common singular. In this second scenario, a *waw* would be reconstructed (*qtlw*) instead of the *taw* required by the first-person form (*qtlt*), creating the indefinite passive "they were killed." Such a reconstruction has grammatical support in both Hebrew and Aramaic. He concludes that J(eh)oram and Ahaziah "were killed," and explicit ownership for the action remains elusive.

> Therefore, it is not justified to seek a historical explanation whereby the author of this text claims to have personally slain Joram and Ahaziah. He may be saying that the two rival kings were assassinated, not by himself, but as an aftermath of his own victories on the field of battle.[23]

Cutting against all these trends, K. Lawson Younger Jr. adopts yet a different approach. Younger assumes the work of M. J. Suriano and Andrew Knapp, who argue that the Tel Dan Stele is an apology on behalf of Hazael.[24] According to Younger, given that the stele "provides legitimation and propaganda for the monarch through a religious explanation for the positive turn of events, crediting the storm God (Hadad)," the answer to the question of who killed the Omride king is either Yahweh or Hadad.[25]

---

23. Rainey and Notley, *Sacred Bridge*, 213. However, Younger has argued that Rainey's proposal goes against "the flow of the narrative." According to Younger, the flow of the narrative seems "to necessitate a first person verbal form" (Younger, "Hazael, Son of a Nobody," 252–53).

24. K. Lawson Younger Jr., *A Political History of the Arameans: From Their Origins to the End of their Polities*, ABS 13 (Atlanta: SBL Press, 2016); see also Andrew Knapp, "Royal Apologetic in the Ancient Near East" (PhD diss., Johns Hopkins University, 2012), later published as *Royal Apologetic in the Ancient Near East*, Writings from the Ancient World Supplement Series 4 (Atlanta: SBL Press, 2015); M. J. Suriano, "The Apology of Hazael: A Literary and Historical Analysis of the Tel Dan Inscription, *JNES* 66 (2007): 163–76.

25. Younger, *Political History of the Arameans*, 613.

Given these divergent proposals, it is undeniable that the socio-political context of the ninth century is also a critical variable. Political relationships were fluid; new territory was being charted. Political pieces were being aggressively moved across the board, and traditional alliances were being challenged. Yet we cannot under-emphasize the literariness of both sources. The genre of the texts is important. Because both the Tel Dan Stele and the biblical account are examples of ancient historiography, they functioned with a certain set of expectations, all of which must be considered. Finally, many of the efforts surveyed here in one way or another focus upon the semantics of *qtl. This highlights the role of language for the discussion. In short, the flexibility of language is an important variable when trying to wade through multiple sources on the way to reconstructing an event.

2.2 HALPERN, HISTORIOGRAPHY, AND LINGUISTIC AMBIGUITY

Baruch Halpern offers a useful framework when considering all the variables that go into assessing ancient historiography. He calls his framework the "Tiglath-Pileser principle," whereby he describes a hermeneutical lens that is particularly important for texts of a royal nature.[26] Some may describe it as a hermeneutic of suspicion, but Halpern prefers the descriptor "minimal interpretation."[27] Either way, he asks the following of these texts: "What is the minimum the king might have done to lay claim to the achievements he publishes?"[28] Indeed, the idea of a minimum standard, versus a fabricated standard, is critical for Halpern: "The point is, such figures cannot make claims without any basis in fact ... lest they invite mockery."[29] Nevertheless,

---

26. Baruch Halpern, *David's Secret Demons: Messiah, Murderer, Traitor, King* (Grand Rapids: Eerdmans, 2001), 124–32.

27. Halpern, *David's Secret Demons*, 131

28. Halpern, *David's Secret Demons*, 126.

29. Halpern, *David's Secret Demons*, 126.

he acknowledges a literary convention that places an "extreme spin on real events."[30]

In explaining his "Tiglath-Pileser principle," Halpern interacts with several Assyrian royal inscriptions. He identifies a literary convention that utilizes periodically occurring summary statements as the critical locus for creating a mighty, infallible impression of the monarch. Yet it is in the details between the summary statements where an informed reader discovers that there is more than meets the eye. Halpern notes the tendency of Tiglath-pileser I to claim total victory in his summary statements, while also acknowledging multiple campaigns, different levels of victory and submission, and varying degrees of tribute in the same account. While this literary convention created the most grandiose triumphs imaginable for the glory of the monarch, it created a significant dynamic that allowed the benefactor to speak out of both sides of his mouth. Thus, the royal rhetoric had to balance an appeal to a general audience—those who absorbed the text uncritically—with an appeal to a more informed audience, who understood the dynamics and methods of historiography, and who could potentially weigh in on the monarch's claims: "The spin, or rhetorical exaggeration, had to be applied within a framework of linguistic conventions that the insiders understood and accepted."[31]

But this method of literary stretching was not confined to Assyrian literature, according to Halpern. He sees evidence of this convention within the Old Testament, particularly Joshua. Joshua 10–11 details varying degrees of "conquest" while the summary statements imply complete conquest (10:41–42; 11:23; 21:43). For example, Joshua "overtook" (לָכַד, lākad) Makkedah, struck it with the edge of the sword (וַיַּכֶּהָ לְפִי־חֶרֶב, wayyakkehā ləpî-ḥerem), and ḥerem-ed every soul in it. He then struck the inhabitants of Libnah with the edge of the sword, and the same fate fell upon King Horam of Gezer and the locations of Eglon, Hebron, and Debir. In every case, Joshua struck the settlement

---

30. Halpern, David's Secret Demons, 126.

31. Halpern, David's Secret Demons, 130.

"with the edge of the sword." In the cases of Hebron, Eglon, and Debir, Joshua fought against it (לָחַם, lāḥam), overtook it (לְכַד, lākad) and even ḥerem-ed it. In 10:40–43, the conquest is ostensibly absolute, subjecting their inhabitants with the prescribed ḥerem. Therefore, according to Halpern, "individual victories metonymically represent the larger conquest" in Joshua.[32] In addition, Halpern believes that 2 Kings 18 employs the principle when discussing Hezekiah's "lordship" over the Philistines. Hezekiah did not control large swaths of Philistine territory. Rather it was his collaboration with other regional polities, which were effective enough to depose a pro-Assyrian monarch, that provided the minimum standard to claim lordship over the region.

Halpern's "Tiglath-Pileser principle" has the benefit of putting the convergence of politics, semantics, public discourse, propaganda, and social issues front and center. It is beyond question that any discussion of royal literature in the ancient world must consider how texts functioned as a political mechanism. And when imperialistic ambitions are added to the equation, such considerations are taken to another level. Yet Halpern's point of emphasis that a kernel of historical reality must be behind the claims of royal literature and that any "egregious falsification" would be out of bounds is critical.[33]

Halpern's commitment to some sort of historical reality behind textual claims appears to stem from his understanding of historiography. As articulated in his previous work *The First Historians*, historiography is the result of antiquarian and systematic interests.[34] Halpern argues that legitimate history writing wants to know what happened, why it is important, and what purpose it bears for contemporary discussion. It seeks to recount the past while simultaneously communicating a particular message. Thus, the pillars of antiquarian and

---

32. Halpern, *David's Secret Demons*, 128. For another important work that contextualizes the Joshua narrative among ancient Near Eastern conquest literature, see K. Lawson Younger Jr., *Ancient Conquest Accounts: A Study in Ancient Near Eastern and Biblical History Writing*, JSOTSup 98 (Sheffield: Sheffield Academic Press, 1990).

33. Halpern, *David's Secret Demons*, 130.

34. Baruch Halpern, *The First Historians: The Hebrew Bible and History* (University Park, PA: University of Pennsylvania Press, 1996), 6–13.

systematic interests exist in a dialectical tension, whereby they push and pull on each other while remaining present and active. In other words, history writing is the result of telling the reader what happened and why it is important by means of creatively using literary conventions of the period in which the historian worked. By implication, therefore, if a claim has no basis in historical reality, then it becomes something other than historiographic writing. Thus, royal historiography, despite its spin, still claims to recount what happened in the life of a monarch. Spin is inherent, as it is a part of the accepted literary canons, but wholesale fabrication fundamentally undermines ancient historiography.

Consequently, Halpern's approach to ancient historiography has important implications for the discussion of the biblical account, the Tel Dan Stele, and who killed off the Omride dynasty. Systematic interests like creativity in presentation, stretching of language, and the exploitation of linguistic ambiguities were all accepted elements of the genre as they helped shape the message intended by the benefactor. However, the antiquarian interests imply that to falsify and/or fabricate events places the account into a non-historiographic literary category. Indeed, it is a delicate balance, but it is both prudent and reasonable to begin with the assumption that there is reality behind both the biblical account and the Tel Dan Stele.

2.3 TOWARD A SYNTHESIS:
BETWEEN TEL DAN, 2 KINGS 9–10, AND BEYOND

It is best to conclude that multiple mechanisms contributed to the downfall of the Omride dynasty. It seems most plausible that both Jehu and Hazael were somehow complicit in the action of ending the dynastic line. As to who assumed the bulk of responsibility in ending said line, it is difficult to say. Clearly the use of *qtl in the Tel Dan Stele is curiously minimalistic, however it is understood. And if Rainey is correct in reading a passive sense, then the semantics are significantly loose. Yet the biblical account also has a curiously ambiguous claim. According to 2 Kings 9:14, "Jehu, son of Jehoshaphat son of Nimshi, conspired against J(eh)oram." The verb *qšr* (קשר) appears in the *hithpael* stem and it too defies any semantic precision. We are not told who was involved but only against whom he conspired. Nevertheless, the biblical account does have the benefit of an expanded narrative (9:1–10:31), and within this narrative the governing dynamics of biblical historiography are exemplified.

2.3.1 BIBLICAL HISTORIOGRAPHY: BETWEEN SYNCHRONY AND DIACHRONY

The biblical account of Jehu's coup begins in 2 Kings 9:1. In the preparatory verses of 9:1–13, we are told that Jehu's efforts are spurred by two factors. First, Elisha the prophet dispatches "one from the sons of the prophets" (לְאַחַד מִבְּנֵי הַנְּבִיאִים, *lə'aḥad mibbnê hannəbî'îm*) to anoint Jehu as the new king. A young prophet (הַנַּעַר הַנָּבִיא, *hannaʿar hannābî'*), who remains unnamed, confronts Jehu while he is among his commanders, eventually anointing him in a back room (9:4–10). As this happens, the prophetic delegate reveals that Jehu's rise to the Israelite throne would function as divine judgment against the Omride family. Thus, Jehu's coup enjoyed divine stimulus and theological reasoning, which was critical for any effort to validate a royal succession that cut against prevailing expectations.

Second, Jehu's colleagues, through their emphatic proclamation of him as king, overwhelm what appears to be an initial lackadaisical attitude toward the news. Initially, Jehu downplays the encounter, responding to the sarcastic inquiry with deflection. The text reads, "When Jehu went out to the servants of his lord, they asked him, 'Is it well? Why did this crazy person come to you?' He said to them, 'You know those guys and their crazy talk'" (2 Kgs 9:11). However, Jehu's colleagues persist, even calling out his deception (9:12). When Jehu finally reveals the details of his encounter with the young prophet, his fellow commanders move to symbolically and publicly proclaim him as king. Jehu in turn quickly secures a capable military force to support his movements, which is another critical variable for securing power. Every ambitious king needs muscle.

The text proceeds to recount in vivid detail Jehu's movements to secure the throne (2 Kgs 9:14–10:31). It is a complex unit that has been subjected to a variety of historical critical investigations. For example, Simon DeVries argues for several stages of redaction, beginning with a prophetic kernel that was incorporated into a Jehuite royal apology and then into the larger Deuteronomistic History while also incurring later scribal glosses.[35] Such historical-critical investigations are potentially important for historical reconstruction. By moving behind the final form of the text, the critic sheds light on the processes by which the biblical account may have developed. In doing so, older layers, layers that would be closer to the events in question, can be identified vis-à-vis newer ones.[36]

However, the difficulties of historical-critical studies are well-known. Any consensus is often elusive, and virtually every conclusion can be criticized for being, at some level, too subjective. Similarly, if there is no consensus from which to begin, any historical reconstruction will be idiosyncratic. Consequently, some scholars are of the opinion that it is best to consider the account of Jehu's coup as a coherent unit. Of those scholars, many see three distinct literary units. First, Jehu is anointed, which established the necessary justification for what follows (2 Kgs 9:1–13). Second, Jehu's actions against the royal leadership are recounted (9:14–31). Finally, Jehu moves to purge the extended family and the remnants of Baalism, all the way down to individual worshipers (10:1–31). In addition, Jehu's death notice appears immediately after these verses, possibly adding a fourth literary unit (10:32–36). Cutting through these sections and giving these

---

35. Simon DeVries, *Prophet against Prophet* (Grand Rapids: Eerdmans, 1978).

36. We are aware that the notion of diachronic studies producing textual layers chronologically closer to the event flirts with historiographic ideas that have been severely criticized in the history of scholarship. Consequently, we emphasize that the importance of diachronic analyses also concerns what can be determined about the contours of the Old Testament's compositional history, any insight toward the intentions or ideology of those that worked to actualize and compile the final form, and any insight toward the total dynamics of divine revelation throughout the Old Testament (see Lawson G. Stone, "On Historical Authenticity, Historical Criticism, and Biblical Authority: Reflections on the Case of the Book of Joshua," *Asbury Theological Journal* 57.2 [2002]: 83–96).

two chapters a distinct sense of coherence are key words, phrases, and literary connections.

Lissa Wray Beal has emphasized the collaboration of the root *šlm (שלם), the verb *nkh (נכה), and the intimate association between the judgment of the Omrides and the judgment of Baalism within 2 Kings 9–10.[37] She points out that the noun šālôm (שָׁלוֹם) occurs ten times in 2 Kings 9–10 (9:11, 17–19, 22, 31; 10:13), while its related verb appears in 9:26. This recurrence creates an overwhelming sense of irony in the narrative, where Jehu's violent and inherently non-šālôm actions are intended to reinstitute šālôm.[38] The use of the verb nkh likewise carries irony. Recurring ten times in 2 Kings 9–10 (9:7, 15, 24, 27; 10:9, 11, 17, 25, 32), it functions throughout as a technical term of judgment. Where Jehu is commanded to strike down the House of Ahab as an act of divine vengeance (9:7), Hazael ironically strikes Israel down (2 Kgs 10:32). Jehu goes from striking down God's adversaries to having his nation struck, but the rationale for this turn of events is found in Jehu's unwillingness to eliminate Jeroboam's illegitimate worship centers (10:28–31).

This account also makes it clear that the judgment of the Omride line is part and parcel with judgment upon Baalism. Clearly, divine judgment upon the Omride family is the overwhelming focus of these two chapters, but as Jehu hunted down the remaining members of the royal family in Samaria the text focuses on Baalism. Through smooth talking and duplicity, Jehu slaughtered the worshipers of Baal by trapping them in their temple, whereby the purging of one led to the purging of the other.

But the artistry of the narrative goes beyond mere irony. In a particularly telling exchange, Jehu stands outside Samaria and proclaims that he intends to "serve" (*ʿbd, עבד) in a way that will surpass the service of Ahab (2 Kgs 10:18). However, his declaration was a ruse to

---

37. Lissa M. Wray Beal, 1 & 2 Kings, AOTC 9 (Downers Grove, IL: InterVarsity Press, 2014), 372–73. The following summary is indebted to Wray Beal's work.

38. Wray Beal relies upon Saul Olyan, "Hăšālôm: Some Literary Considerations of 2 Kings 9," Catholic Biblical Quarterly 46.4 (1984): 652–68.

incite the proponents of Baalism to reveal themselves. According to the narrator in 10:19, Jehu sought to "destroy" (*ʾbd, אבד) them, creating a pun between the verbs *ʾbd and *ʿbd.[39] The paronomastic element demonstrates the artistry embedded in the historical account, an element found also in Jezebel's greeting of Jehu immediately preceding her death. She greets Jehu by the wrong name, Zimri, an unmistakable swipe at Jehu. By calling him Zimri, one of the shortest-lived kings in Israel, it could be that Jezebel revealed some wishful thinking. Essentially, "May Jehu's reign also be incredibly short." Also possible is an overt connection between their positions as generals and usurpers.[40] Either way, the artistry of the account is on full display.

Consequently, when a synchronic reading is preferred, a reading that does not concern itself with any reconstructed, pre-final form, it is clear that 2 Kings 9–10 is well crafted and laced with a palpable level of artistry. More importantly, the flow of the account progresses to a stimulating climax. The zealous usurper and the one who purged the Omride dynasty and Baalism from Israel failed to purge the one religious influence that was at the root of Israel's problems: Jeroboam's sanctuaries at Bethel and Dan (10:28–31). However, Nathan Lovell has argued that endurance of the sanctuaries is not something for which Jehu is culpable.[41] Regardless, the presentation is deliberate, whereby the realities of Jehu's coup are presented as a cog in a larger theological assessment.

Ultimately, this sheds light on perhaps the biggest difficulty in utilizing the biblical accounts for historical reconstruction: the synchrony and diachrony of the text as well as the relationship between the two. On the one hand, it is indubitable that there is a textual history behind the biblical source material. What constitutes the source's final form

---

39. So, Wray Beal, *1 & 2 Kings*, 380.

40. Nathan Lovell, *The Books of Kings and Exilic Identity: 1 and 2 Kings as a Work of Political Historiography*, LHBOTS 708 (New York: T&T Clark, 2021), 62–64.

41. For Lovell 1 Kgs 13:1–3 and 2 Kgs 10:30 are important. Here, Josiah is identified as the solution for the problematic sanctuaries and Jehu is praised for his purge. Moreover, Lovell's understanding of Jehu is framed by a sophisticated narrative analogy between Jehu and Zimri (Lovell, *Kings and Exilic Identity*, 72, 141–43).

is very often the result of a lengthy and complicated process of textual composition and development. On the other hand, the biblical material urges a synchronic reading as it currently exists in a unified narrative. So, how is one to navigate between these two qualities? For the purposes of historical reconstruction, should the critic disregard synchronic readings in preference of historical critical methods of study as able to answer historical questions more effectively? Or is there a method of historical inquiry that moves between synchronic and diachronic perspectives, utilizing the historical value of both postures?

In response, Wray Beal, Lovell, and others cogently explain how a synchronic reading of 2 Kings 9–10 sheds light on the elements inherent to Jehu's coup and reign, so much so that such a reading implies that the dynamics of Jehu's coup and reign are more important than any historical questions about Jehu's relationship to Aram or whether he was actively responsible for the end of the Omrides. Yet the likely clausal resumption (*Wiederaufnahme*) between 8:29 and 9:15 qualifies any synchronic reading. The very presence of this well-known scribal convention, which draws the reader's attention to an insertion, urges the historian to engage in historical-critical analyses, despite their difficulty and tenuousness.[42] If the Israelite account of Jehu's coup existed at one time without prophetic sanction (9:1–13), and was colored by an ambiguous claim of conspiracy (9:14), then it was understood at one point to be a coup born more out of political ambitions, rather than divine sanction and prophetic support.

This is not to say that an earlier understanding of the events rejected the notion of collusion between Aram and Jehu. It merely implies that the Israelite account was initially focused on the actions of Jehu. Yet the inserted materials that anchor Jehu's coup in divine

---

42. On this methodological point, see the implications of Serge Frolov below. On the issue of *Wiederaufnahme* as a scribal marker highlighting editorial activity, Bernard M. Levinson has provided a useful summary, noting "[t]he repetitive resumption brackets a digression or interpolation by framing it with a repetition. One or two clauses from the material preceding the interruption are repeated after it to mark the resumption of the original text" (Levinson, "The Hermeneutics of Innovation: The Impact of Centralization upon the Structure, Sequence, and Reformulation of Legal Material in Deuteronomy" [PhD diss., Brandeis University, 1991], 146).

sanction and admit a level of conspiracy provide a later understanding that further justifies the coup and explains in more detail the historical circumstances around the event. Collusion between Jehu and Aram was apparently accepted as a more palatable explanation of the events.

2.3.2 ARTICULATING A METHOD

The discussion about moving between synchronic and diachronic perspectives has far-reaching implications. Above all, when engaging in historical reconstruction one must consider the sources. When reconstructing elements of Omride history, inscriptions are particularly important, as is demonstrated throughout this work. But inscriptions are not always historical narratives, and they present their own set of variables. For example, establishing a readable text is regularly a pressing concern when dealing with inscriptions.[43] And as Lester Grabbe has emphasized, propagandistic statements as well as legitimate and illegitimate references also need to be anticipated and critically assessed.[44] For biblical sources this process is incredibly complex. First, each individual episode must be critically evaluated in light of the overarching historical concerns of the book in which it appears, whereby that agenda affects the way individual elements are recounted, whether it be Kings, Chronicles, or any other book. The whole affects the sum of its parts. But more importantly, the biblical episodes must be considered in light of pertinent diachronic issues, for the process of textual development may have something to say. Additionally, diachronic issues are not created equally and must be considered on a case-by-case basis.[45]

Yet this does not mean that, when warranted, a governing rubric for moving between synchronic and diachronic perspectives is too

---

43. This is not to say that the biblical accounts are absent of any textual issues. As we shall see, textual issues are relevant in the biblical source material.

44. Lester L. Grabbe, "Reflections on the Discussion," in Grabbe, *Ahab Agonistes*, 339. Again, this is not to say that such perspectives do not appear in the biblical account. Rather, the extent and dynamics of these possibilities are the essence of the historiographic debate.

45. Grabbe, "Reflections," 340.

problematic to articulate. The opposite is true. A governing rubric is critical, but it needs to be malleable enough to accommodate the unique variables of each situation. Serge Frolov has spoken usefully on this issue. According to Frolov, the shift between synchronic and diachronic perspectives "may not be arbitrary," and it "must be warranted."[46] Warrant appears when literary phenomena, such as doublets, repetitions, grammatical and syntactical difficulties, and other realities, reach a certain qualitative and/or quantitative threshold. That point is called a bifurcation point, the point when the critic is compelled to shift from a synchronic posture to a diachronic posture. So, in the example mentioned above, the clausal resumption between 2 Kings 8:29 and 9:15 appears to constitute that bifurcation point.

In addition, no matter the source, it is prudent to consider the semantic possibilities vis-à-vis the semantic demands. The historian must consider what is both grammatically possible and grammatically impossible. By considering what is *grammatically* possible and impossible, *historical* possibilities, which are critical for historical reconstruction, may be discovered. For example, in the critical historical question of who ended the Omride dynasty, the debate was initially framed by the assumption that *qtl was to be understood in the active sense. Such a parameter restricted the debate. Yet as Rainey argued, it is very possible to read a passive form of *qtl. And if the passive voice is accepted, the possibilities for a historical reconstruction increase. In fact, a passive reading bolsters the reconstructions offered by Schniedewind, Kottsieper, and others who suggest some form of collusion between Jehu and Aram.

The point is this. Historical reconstruction is not a robotic endeavor, as if inputting a certain number of variables will always produce the answer. As Grabbe emphasizes, historical reconstruction involves judgment, creativity, imagination, a commitment—not slavish—to guidelines, and a willingness to reconsider conclusions in light of

---

46. Serge Frolov, *The Turn of the Cycle: 1 Samuel 1–8 in Synchronic and Diachronic Perspectives*, BZAW 342 (Berlin: Walter de Gruyter, 2004), 31–32.

new evidence or understandings.[47] Consequently, this project will proceed and employ the guidelines discussed hitherto. We seek to reconstruct the military conflicts of the Omride dynasty. What is more, we seek to demonstrate that the biblical sources and the Levantine/ Mesopotamian sources are complementary, not mutually exclusive, testimonies to the historical realities of the ninth century BC.[48]

As argued in this chapter, the Tel Dan Stele and the biblical account of 2 Kings 9–10 can be synthesized, but it begins with recognizing the objectives and dynamics inherent to each source. Together, both sources speak to what happened, revealing a variety of mechanisms that brought down the Omride dynasty. Aramean aggression, ambitious factions within the military, the political maneuvering of prophetic elements, and the physical weakness of the sitting Omride king all converged to create a perfect storm.

The following historical sketch of the ninth century BC establishes the backdrop for the rest of this study. As will be seen, the situation was incredibly fluid, dictated by the imperialistic ambitions of the fledgling Neo-Assyrian Empire.

2.4 A HISTORICAL SKETCH OF THE NINTH CENTURY BC

To put it succinctly, the Levant of the ninth century was shaped largely by the ambitions of Assyria. While Babylon was a constant nuisance to the Assyrians, it lacked the organization and charismatic figures necessary to become a significant force. According to David Vanderhooft, this period in Babylonian history was "rather unremarkable," where "few Babylonian kings emerge into sharp focus, and their dynastic affiliations remain mostly unknown."[49] Similarly in Egypt,

---

47. Grabbe, "Reflections," 340.

48. While the biblical accounts ostensibly derive from a Levantine provenance, we are drawing a distinction between biblical and extrabiblical texts. Thus, by "Levantine," we refer to the non-biblical texts from Syria and Moab.

49. David S. Vanderhooft, "Babylonia and the Babylonians," in *The World around the Old Testament*, ed. Bill T. Arnold and Brent A. Strawn (Grand Rapids: Baker Academic, 2016), 123.

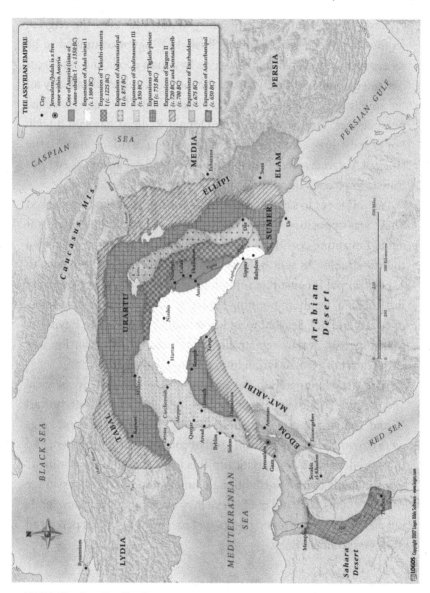

MAP 1: **The Assyrian Empire**

Dynasty 22 proved to lack any "unity of purpose" after the reign of its founder Shoshenq I (biblical Shishak).[50] Egypt continued to be an economic force, particularly since Egyptian goods and resources remained attractive. Yet Dynasty 22 found it difficult to sustain any initial ambitions and failed to overcome internal rebellions and parochial perspectives. On the whole then, Donald Redford has said it well: "For exactly three centuries from the ascension of Adad-nirari II, the story of Assyria is one of almost uninterrupted expansion as Assyria transformed itself into the scourge of the ancient world."[51]

Yet this is not to say that Assyria's march to Egypt went unchecked. There was opposition to Assyrian advances, particularly from formidable Levantine coalitions. Such coalitions, however, only delayed the inevitable. As will be described, the efforts of the Assyrian Ashurnasirpal II constitute something like Julius Caesar's crossing of the Rubicon, firmly committing the Neo-Assyrian Empire to a series of events and policies that would eventually bring them to Egypt. As Mario Liverani has systematically argued, territorial expansion was at the heart of Neo-Assyrian imperialistic ideology.[52]

The Assyrian march to the African continent had its ideological and practical foundations in the policies of Ashur-dan II, Adad-nirari II, and Tukulti-Ninurta II. As described by Amelié Kuhrt, these kings were convinced of a significant level of continuity between them and their predecessors. Militaristically, this translated into regular incursions in lands that were traditionally understood to be Assyrian territories.[53] Thus, they did not believe they were conquering new lands but rather were suppressing perpetual revolts in what was perceived to be Assyrian territory.

---

50. Donald Redford, *Egypt, Canaan, and Israel in Ancient Times* (Princeton: Princeton University Press, 1992), 315.

51. Redford, *Egypt, Canaan, and Israel*, 338.

52. Mario Liverani, *Assyria: The Imperial Mission*, trans. Andrea Trameri and Jonathan Valk (Winona Lake, IN: Eisenbrauns, 2017), 41–54.

53. Amelié Kuhrt, *The Ancient Near East, c. 3000–330 BC*, 2 vols. (London: Routledge, 1997), 2:479.

TABLE 2: Ninth-century reigns[54]

Aram-Damascus		Judah		Israel		Neo-Assyria	
c. 900–880	Ben-Hadad I					911–891	Adad-nirari II
						890–884	Tukulti-Ninurta II
c. 880–844/43	Ben-Hadad II (Hadad-ezer)	913–873	Asa	876–869	Omri	883–859	Ashurnasirpal II
		873–849	Jehoshaphat	869–850	Ahab		
844/43–803	Hazael	849–842	J(eh)oram	850–849	Ahaziah	859–824	Shalmaneser III
		842	Ahaziah	849–842	J(eh)oram		
		842–837	Athaliah	842–815	Jehu	823–811	Shamshi-Adad V
c. 803–775	Ben-Hadad III (Mari ?)	837–800	Jehoash	815–801	Joahaz	810–783	Adad-nirari III

54. This table adapts Kuhrt's chronology (Kuhrt, *Ancient Near East*, 2:468, 479) and Younger's "Aram-Damascus Kings List" (Younger, *Political History of the Arameans*, 653). Kuhrt relies upon Albright for coordinating Israelite and Judean reigns (William F. Albright, "The Chronology of the Divided Monarchy," *BASOR* 100 [1945]: 16–22).

In this context, Assyria's northern borders were critical as a breach offered efficient access into the heart of Assyrian territory. Consequently, a large percentage of Assyrian resources were devoted to securing this border. However, there were conflicts with Aramean groups, particularly along the western edge of these boundaries. In response, the policies of Adad-nirari II appear to initiate an Assyrian ideological shift. By engaging in at least eight campaigns against the Arameans in the vicinity of the western arm of the Euphrates River, he signaled the re-allocation of resources to expanding the western border, as opposed to fortifying the northern borders.[55] Nevertheless, it was not until the reign of Ashurnasirpal II that Assyria made an aggressive effort to redefine the traditional understanding of Assyrian control in the ancient Near East.

The reign of Ashurnasirpal is described as one of "relentless warfare" as military expansion and general conflict became the chief mechanism for advancing his political agenda.[56] Indeed, he created policy that Assyria must enact at least one yearly military campaign. He also transformed a relatively insignificant village, Kalhu (Nimrud; biblical Calah), into one of the great imperial centers of the ancient world and into a symbol of military aggression and political hegemony. Kalhu showcased a massive complex dedicated to Ninurta, the god of war. Pragmatically, the king was utterly ruthless in maintaining order, and some accounts recall the sacking of cities punctuated by subjecting the rebellious to a public and gruesome death as a deterrent. For example, Ashurnasirpal recounts a particularly gruesome reaction to the rebellious city of Surus.

> With my staunch heart and fierce weapons I besieged the city. All of the guilty soldiers were seized and handed over to me. ... I appointed Azi-ili as my own governor over them. I erected a pile in front of his gate; I flayed as many nobles as (i 90) had rebelled against me (and) draped their skins over the pile; some

---

55. Rainey and Notley, *Sacred Bridge*, 190.
56. Rainey and Notley, *Sacred Bridge*, 190.

I spread out within the pile, some I erected on stakes upon the pile, (and) some I placed on stakes around the pile. I flayed many right through my land (and) draped their skins over the walls. I slashed the flesh of the eunuchs (and) of the royal eunuchs who were guilty. I brought Aḫi-iababa to Nineveh, flayed him, (and) draped his skin over the wall of Nineveh.[57]

Between 875 and 867 BC, Ashurnasirpal progressed beyond the traditional eastern, western, and northern boundaries to engage new territories, especially those west of the Euphrates River. Eventually, he "washed" his weapons in the Mediterranean Sea, which represented a pivotal moment in Assyrian history.

At that time I made my way to the slopes of Mount Lebanon (and) went up to the Great Sea of the land Amurru. I cleansed my weapons in the Great Sea (and) made sacrifices to the gods. I received tribute from the kings of the sea coast, from the lands of the people of Tyre, Sidon, Byblos, Mahallatu, Maizu, Kaizu, Amurru, and the city Arvad which is (on an island) in the sea. … They submitted to me.[58]

In the end, Ashurnasirpal left huge shoes to fill. Amazingly, Shalmaneser III had the feet to fill them. Described as a "fitting sequel," he intensified the aggressive policies of his father, penetrating deeper into Syria-Palestine. Yet Shalmaneser III's movements into Syria-Palestine were anything but smooth. Rather, they were more like waves slowly progressing further onto shore during a rising tide.[59] Initial efforts were met with resistance, which may or may not have worked.[60] But with each subsequent effort Assyria was able to

---

57. Ashurnasirpall II A.0.101.1, i 82b–93a (RIMA 2:199).

58. Ashurnasirpall II A.0.101.1, iii 84b–88a (RIMA 2:218–19).

59. A. Kirk Grayson, RIMA 3:5.

60. Royal inscriptions are notoriously difficult to interpret. The reader must read between the lines and peel back layers of rhetoric designed to deflect and focus the audience upon a particular message.

FIGURE 2: **A relief of Shalmaneser III**

systematically erode the efficacy of the Syro-Palestinian coalitions.
Therefore, resistance was relatively short-lived and absorption into
the Assyrian Empire was only a matter of time as the region was
overwhelmed by either the might of the Assyrians or by the hostilities

between coalition members. Nevertheless, the precise nature of Shalmaneser's conflicts is always difficult to discern, for the rhetorical flair of the Assyrian records is difficult to penetrate. Indeed, polities that apparently suffered the wrath of his supposed total victory continued to function with some autonomy after the fact.[61]

The battle of Qarqar (853 BC) was a particularly important event for Shalmaneser, which occurred in the sixth year of his reign. It must be understood in the context of the king's efforts to maintain order across his kingdom and continue the ambitious policies of his predecessor Ashurnasirpal. The Kurkh Monolith Inscription and other accounts recount how Shalmaneser received the tribute of Aleppo without a fight, and how he eventually arrived at Qarqar.[62] On his way there, several cities suffered the wrath of the aggravated Assyrian monarch, but at Qarqar he faced a formidable coalition from the Syro-Palestinian region. Both Ahab and the Aramean Adad-idri (biblical Hadad-ezer) were members of the coalition, and both contributed largely to the coalition force. However, according to the Kurkh Monolith, the "supreme forces" of Assyria "decisively defeated" the coalition. More specifically, there is a claim to have burned Qarqar to the ground, chased members of the coalition in retreat, seized their chariotry forces, braggadociously littered the ground with corpses, blocked the Orontes River with bodies, and formed rivers of blood.[63]

This battle is significant for at least two reasons. First, it demonstrates that Israel and Aram-Damascus were leading polities united against a common enemy. According to figures in Shalmaneser's report, the Aramean Adad-idri (Hebrew: Hadad-ezer) contributed 1,200 chariots, 1,200 calvary, and 20,000 troops. Ahab contributed 2,000 chariots and 10,000 infantry. Incidentally, these figures surpass

61. For example, Shalmaneser boasts that in his tenth regnal year he faced off against Hadad-ezer and the rest of the Syro-Palestinian coalition, defeating them and seizing their military implements in the wake of their shameful retreat. Yet the very next year, he apparently faced the same coalition with the same results (Shalmaneser III A.0.102.6, ii.55–iii.15 [RIMA 3:37–38]).

62. "Kurkh Monolith," trans. K. Lawson Younger Jr. (COS 2.113A:261–64); Shalmaneser III A.0.102.2, ii.86b–89a (RIMA 3:23–24).

63. "Kurkh Monolith," ii. 86b–102 (COS 2.113A:263).

the contributions of the other coalition members. Second, the battle of Qarqar constitutes a critical point in establishing a timeline of Shalmaneser's advance across the region. Moreover, as we will immediately see, his engagement with the Syro-Palestinian region was tremendously erratic, often separated by years of absence. During these windows of absence, traditional rivalries and hostilities among certain Syro-Palestinian polities metastasized.

The Kurkh Monolith ends abruptly after recounting the maneuvers at Qarqar, implying that Shalmaneser's bombastic claims were compensating for failure. In reality, the consensus of scholars believes this to be the case, and so one can say that the inscription is likely reflecting the "Tiglath-Pileser principle" (see above), emphatically touting Assyria's superior forces and the coalition's battlefield casualties in order to shift focus away from the coalition's success in repelling his advances. Moreover, Shalmaneser's subsequent campaigns into Syria-Palestine are similarly calculated. He does not cross the western arm of the Euphrates River to engage the coalition again until his tenth year, which was then followed by other campaigns during his eleventh and fourteenth years. This timeline suggests that the coalition parlayed their initial victory into subsequent successes.[64] In other words, the Assyrian march toward Egypt became a campaign of attrition, sustained over decades and many administrations with varying results. Nevertheless, in his eighteenth year, Shalmaneser claims to meet Hazael of Damascus, whom he dispatched on his way to the mountains of Ba'li-rasi where he erected a statue of himself.[65] Consequently, the eighteenth year appears to have been a critical point in his tenure, for this is also the context in which Jehu offers him tribute, famously memorialized on the Black Obelisk.[66]

---

64. "Annals: Assur Clay Tablets," trans. K. Lawson Younger Jr. (*COS* 2.113B:264–266). While Hadad-ezer is mentioned in these accounts, there is no mention of an Israelite force.

65. This is an unknown location that some have identified with Mt. Carmel (see "Annals: Calah Bulls," trans. K. Lawson Younger Jr. [*COS* 2.113C:267 n. 4]).

66. "The Black Obelisk," trans. K. Lawson Younger Jr. (*COS* 2.113F:269–270); see also "Annals: Calah Bulls" (*COS* 2.113C); "Annals: Marble Slab," trans. K. Lawson Younger Jr. (*COS* 2.113D:267–268); "Kurba'il Statue," trans. K. Lawson Younger Jr. (*COS* 2.113E:268–269).

FIGURE 3: **The Black Obelisk of Shalmaneser III, depicting vassal kings bringing tribute**

After Shalmaneser III, Assyrian dominance waned. At the end of the ninth century, Shamshi-Adad V and then Adad-nirari III assumed the throne, and they both struggled to fulfill the policies of Shalmaneser. In the case of Adad-nirari, a telling relationship with his mother may have also affected his ability to fulfill the imperialistic ambitions of his predecessors.[67] Unfortunately, the reigns of both Shamshi-Adad and Adad-nirari are plagued by a relative lack of documentation. Amelié Kuhrt describes a steady decline in Assyrian influence until the reign of Tiglath-pileser III.[68] This Assyrian decline ultimately allowed Hazael, king of Aram-Damascus, to construct a kingdom that came to dominate the region.

Explaining the historical developments of the Arameans and Aram-Damascus is complicated. Fundamentally, the term "Arameans" refers to separate tribal groups that were linked linguistically, through a common use of Aramaic, and a general pattern of social transition. Birthed out of a normadic way of life, Aramean polities eventually became sedentary. Exactly how this transition unfolded is an important part of the conversation. Traditionally, it has been explained by a process of migration, invasion, or some type of symbiotic process.[69] However, in light of an increasing awareness about the end of the Late Bronze Age, a collapse model has also developed.[70] Essentially, the Arameans moved away from nomadism in conjunction with opportunities offered in the wake of this systems-collapse.[71] In the end, the best explanation will undoubtedly contain multiple elements, for monolithic explanations fail to account for complex historical realities.

---

67. Adad-nirari's mother was Sammu-Rāmat. Upon the death of her husband Shamshi-Adad V, she appears to have assumed the throne as a bridge between her husband and their son. From what can be reconstructed, she ostensibly functioned effectively and enjoyed a legacy celebrated by later iconic cultures of the ancient world. When she eventually yielded to Adad-nirari, her influence continued, where she even accompanied him on the battlefield. In one instance, responsibility is given to both Sammu-Rāmat and Adad-nirari for erecting a monument in response to a military campaign west of the Euphrates. For discussion see Saana Svärd, *Women and Power in Neo-Assyrian Palaces*, Neo-Assyrian Text Corpus Project (Winona Lake, IN: Eisenbrauns, 2015); Saano Teppo, "Agency and the Neo-Assyrian Women of the Palace," *Studia Orientalia* 101 (2007): 381–420, esp. 390.

68. Kuhrt, *Ancient Near East*, 2:492.

69. Younger, *Political History of the Arameans*, 63–68.

70. Younger, *Political History of the Arameans*, 68–70.

71. For an accessible definition of "systems-collapse" and the dynamics of the Late Bronze Age collapse, see Eric H. Cline, *1177 B.C.: The Year Civilization Collapsed*, Turning Points in Ancient History 2 (Princeton: Princeton University Press, 2015), esp. 160–70.

FIGURE 4: **A stele of the Assyrian queen Sammu-Rāmat**

The origin of Aramean culture appears to have revolved around three general geographic regions. Younger argues that Aramean polities found their focus in Hittite, Assyrian, and central and southern Levant regions.[72] In turn, certain Aramean polities were able to assert themselves over others. In the case of the first two regions, Aramean

---

72. Concisely, K. Lawson Younger Jr., "Aram and the Arameans," in *The World around the Old Testament*, ed. Bill T. Arnold and Brent A. Strawn (Grand Rapids: Baker Academic, 2019), 238–43; more extensively, Younger, *Political History of the Arameans*, 109–220.

developments were complicated by their proximity to the empires of
Hatti and Assyria. The accounts of Ashur-dan II, Adad-nirari II, and
Tukulti-Ninurta II all speak of beating back Aramean contingencies
as they continued their eastward movement, a movement made possible by the relative ineffectiveness of Assyria during the tenth century
BC.[73] With respect to the Levantine regions, the Arameans had to
contend with small but capable polities, including Israel. David had
conflicts with the Arameans (2 Sam 8:3–10; 10), and Rezon, one of
Solomon's adversaries, broke away from Hadad-ezer of Zobah[74] to
recruit a band of marauders that settled in Damascus and made life
generally difficult for the Israelite king (1 Kgs 11:23–25).

The location of Rezon's Damascus remains impossible to identify
due to a variety of socio-political factors that prevent proper archaeological expeditions. Similarly, virtually all extant inscriptions that shed
light on the issue were found in secondary usage, requiring careful
qualification. Nevertheless, Younger argues for the beginnings of the
Aram-Damascus polity in the vicinity of the al-Ghutah oasis, currently a residential and industrial suburb outside of the modern city
of Damascus. From al-Ghutah, the polity expanded southward and
northeast, eventually encompassing the cities of Yabrudu, Haurina,
Danabu, Malahia, Ashtara, Gal'ad, Metuna, Kurussa, Qarinu, Samaya,
and Mansuate.[75]

Developing a king list of those ruling Aram-Damacus is also
notoriously difficult. According to 1 Kings 15:18–20, the king of
Aram-Damascus during the reigns of Asa and Baasha was ostensibly Ben-Hadad I, who is described as the "son of Tabrimmon son
of Hezrion" (15:18). However, "Ben-Hadad" appears in other locations as well (1 Kgs 20; 2 Kgs 6:24; 8; 13), suggesting the possibility

73. Aššur-dān II A.0.98, Adad-nārārī II A.0.99, Tikultī-Ninurta A.0.100 (RIMA 2:131–88).

74. Zobah was likely located along the west side of the Anti-Lebanon Mountains, perhaps
north of the Beqa Valley (Carl G. Rasmussen, *Zondervan Atlas of the Bible*, rev. ed. [Grand
Rapids: Zondervan, 2010], 140).

75. See Younger, *Political History of the Arameans*, 557–64.

of three different Aramean kings named Ben-Hadad.[76] As if this was not confusing enough, Assyrian sources reference Aramean kings by different names. In a well-known example, Ahab's contemporary was known not as Ben-Hadad II (see 1 Kgs 20) but as Adad-idri. However, Adad-idri (biblical Hadad-ezer) is not linguistically compatible with Ben-Hadad, a tension that has not only produced robust commentary but also has called into question the historical veracity of the biblical account. Nevertheless, it is reasonable to understand the name Ben-Hadad, which literally means "son of Hadad," as a generic title employed by the biblical writer. Whereas the Assyrian historians referenced Aramean kings by name, the Israelite historian was content with a general reference.[77] More will be said about this in the following chapter.

One king of Aram-Damascus whose identification is inscrutable is Hazael. While it is relatively clear that he usurped the throne somewhere between 844 and 842 BC, it remains unclear how close he was to the legitimate line of succession. Based on the Assyrian description that he was a "son of nobody" (mār lā mammāna),[78] as well as the apologetic nature of the Tel Dan Stele (see above), Hazael likely altered the natural line of succession. The book of Kings bears

---

76. The factors leading to two or three Ben-Hadads ruling Aram-Damascus are contingent upon how one understands the length of reigns and/or the redactional history behind the Elijah/Elisha narratives. We discuss this in greater detail in chapter 3.

77. Younger provides a cogent explanation for this difficulty, with tentative conclusions. Recognizing the dubiousness of equating Ben-Hadad with Hadad-ezer, and of accepting that 1 Kings 20, 22, and 2 Kings 8:7–15 betray a perspective from the time of Jehu, Younger privileges the Assyrian records due to their preference for Aramean names rather than honorifics: "It seems very possible that Ben-Hadad was a dynastic name. ... Hence in this instance, Ben-Hadad appears to have been used as an honorific, expressing adoption language" (Younger, *Political History of the Arameans*, 580–84, esp. 584).

78. Most famously on the Assur Basalt Statue (Shalmaneser III A.0.102.40, i.25–ii.6 [RIMA 3:118]). Strictly speaking, *lā mamman* simply means "not anyone" (see examples in *CAD* 10.1:195–98). The collocation *lā mamman* is also used in a derogatory manner to connote illegitimacy, as indicated by the presence of a certain appositional phrase *la bēl* ⁱˢˢⁱkussê, "who had no authority to the throne." For more on *lā mamman* in the Assyrian King List, see Kyle R. Greenwood, "Assyrian King List," in *The Ancient Near East: Historical Sources in Translation*, ed. Mark W. Chavalas (Oxford: Blackwell, 2006): 368–72, esp. 371; M. B. Rowton, "Tuppu and the Date of Hammurabi," *JNES* 10.3 (1951): 184–204, esp. 198.

witness to this, describing Hazael as a member of the royal court who asphyxiated the sitting Aramean king (2 Kgs 8:7–15). Ironically, Hazael would watch over the Golden Age of Aram-Damascus.

In 841 BC, Shalmaneser III first faced off against Hazael in the context of his Syro-Palestinian campaigns. On the Marble Slab he boasts about chasing Hazael from his mountain fortress back to Damascus.[79] However, the dynamics of Shalmaneser's victory are called into question. In 838 BC he confronted Hazael for the last time. As attested on the Black Obelisk, the Assyrian claims to have captured four of Hazael's fortified cities, but nowhere does Shalmaneser mention sacking Aram-Damascus or relieving Hazael of his kingship. This is a significant lacuna in the Assyrian account, for as suggested by Halpern, even royal rhetoric has its limits suggesting that the center of Aramean power remained intact and was capable of quick resurgence.

As Shalmaneser III gave way to Shamshi-Adad V and Adad-nirari III, Hazael seized his opportunity to rebuild Aram-Damascus and to assert his dominance throughout the southern Levant. According to Younger, Hazael wrested strategic portions of Gilead from Israelite control (2 Kgs 10:32–33), made incursions into Israelite territory, and even moved toward Judah and Jerusalem in conjunction with his efforts to control Philistine land (12:18).[80] In contrast, Matthieu Richelle appeals to textual variations in the Septuagintal traditions, arguing that Hazael consumed the majority of the Transjordanian region, suggesting that Aramean interest in the coastal plain is the product of textual corruption.[81] Either way, it is unquestionable that Hazael was able to assert Aramean dominance throughout Syria-Palestine at the end of the ninth century in the wake of Assyrian weakening. It is no wonder that Elisha wept before Hazael's reign (8:10–13).

---

79. "Annals: Marble Slab" (*COS* 2.113D:267–268).

80. Younger, *Political History of the Arameans*, 620–30.

81. Matthieu Richelle, "Les conquetes de Hazael selon la recension lucianique en 4 Regnes 13,22," *BN* 146 (2010): 19–25.

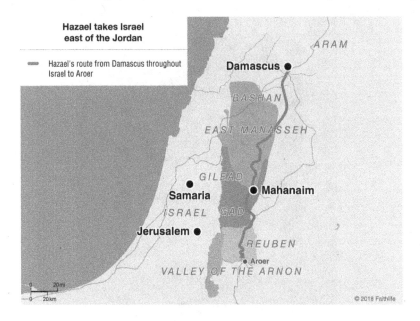

MAP 2: **Hazael takes Israel east of the Jordan**

Nevertheless, the dominance of Aram-Damascus was relatively short-lived as it was unable to sustain its prominence after Hazael. Ben-Hadad III appears in 2 Kings 13:3, 24–25, as well as the Zakkur Inscription, but it is clear that he struggled to exert the same dominance. Zakkur testifies that Bar-Hadad (biblical Ben-Hadad) brought a coalition of seventeen kings against the king of Hamath and Luash but failed to produce a successful siege.[82] Similarly, Jehoash, king of Israel, reclaimed traditionally held territory from Ben-Hadad III (13:24–25). Finally, Adad-nirari III claims to have confined Hazael's successor to Damascus while securing his tribute and vassalship.[83] Thus, "from roughly 803 to 796, Damascus had gone from the most powerful kingdom in the Levant to a much-weakened kingdom, one

---

82. "The Inscription of Zakkur, King of Hamath," trans. Allan Millard (*COS* 2.35:155).

83. "Calah Orthostat Slab," trans. K. Lawson Younger Jr. (*COS* 2.114G:276–277).

FIGURE 5: **The Zakkur Inscription**

that now faced potential losses in the southern territories, namely to a renewed Israel under Joash/Jehoash."[84]

2.5 CONCLUSIONS

The historical realities surveyed here describe a period characterized by a significant level of socio-political fluidity. The imperialistic ideals of the Assyrians, which crystalized with Ashur-dan II but were taken to new levels with Ashurnasirpal II and Shalmaneser III, dictated the

84. Younger, *Political History of the Arameans*, 635.

actions of smaller polities in Syria-Palestine. However, when Assyria chose to devote their resources to other territorial fronts, and certainly when their dominance began to wane, these polities felt free to reconsider their relationships with each other. In certain instances, reconsiderations resurrected traditional hostilities. Thus, while the Assyrian threat, most prominently in the form of Shalmaneser's military campaigns, initially facilitated cooperation between Israelite and Aramean polities, such cooperation was tenuous at best. And if Hess's invocation of the Mari archives as offering precedent is at all instructive, the waning of any external pressure could be enough to allow regional hostilities to resume between Israel and Aram-Damascus.[85]

---

85. Hess invokes Wolfgang Heimpel's reconstruction of West Semitic alliances as evidence that they could be redrawn and that traditional hostilities could be resurrected quickly: "Heimpel notes the alliance between Mari, Babylon, Ekallatum, and other states that was so strong when threatened by the outside power of Elam, disintegrated within months of the removal of that threat. Mari and Ekallatum became antagonists" (Richard Hess, Review of *Letters to the King of Mari: A New Translation, with Historical Introduction, Notes, and Commentary*, by Wolfgang Heimpel, *Denver Journal* 8 [2005]: n.p.; see Wolfgang Heimpel, *Letters to the King of Mari: A New Translation, with Historical Introduction, Notes, and Commentary*, Mesopotamian Civilizations 12 [Winona Lake, IN: Eisenbrauns, 2003], 130; see also Greenwood, "Late Tenth- and Ninth-Century Issues," 311).

Chapter 3

THE SIEGE OF SAMARIA

F irst Kings 20 begins with an abrupt shift from the material that precedes it. The dynamics between the prophetic and royal institutions give way to Israelite/Aramean relations. Moreover, this shift also brings an ominous tone to the larger narrative. According to the first verse, the Aramean king, identified only as Ben-Hadad (בֶּן־הֲדַד, *ben-hădad*, "son of Hadad"), gathered thirty-two kings for a formidable military coalition to besiege Samaria. However, the specific impetus for engaging in such a siege is never disclosed. The reader is merely told that Ben-Hadad of Aram and his coalition besiege Samaria, and these factors cooperate to feed a robust debate on the historical context assumed by 1 Kings 20 and 22 (see below).[1]

In the context of 1 Kings 20, Aram and its coalition are presented as the aggressor. Moreover, Israel assumes a posture behind the walls of their city, suggesting an inferior position. Consequently, when the Israelite king initially accepts the terms dispatched by the Aramean king, there is little surprise:

---

1. For a concise survey of the historical challenges associated with 1 Kings 20 and 22, see Greenwood, "Late Tenth- and Ninth-Century Issues," 306.

And they said to him, "Thus says Ben-Hadad, 'Your silver and your gold are mine; your women and your best sons, they are mine.'" The king of Israel answered, "According to your word, my lord, O king. I am yours, as well as everything which belongs to me." (1 Kgs 20:3–4)

What is intriguing is the Aramean response to Israel's acceptance of terms. With little indication of how much time elapsed, Ben-Hadad re-dispatched his envoy to adjust his terms, informing the Israelite king that he must prepare the city for looting:

Then the messengers returned and said, "Thus says Ben-Hadad, 'Indeed I dictated to you that you would give me your silver, your gold, your wives, and your sons. Yet at this time tomorrow I will send my servants to you so that they might search your house and the house of your servants. Everything that is precious in your eyes they will put in their hands so that they may take it.'" (1 Kgs 20:5–6)

Such intensification contributes to the characterization of Ben-Hadad as arrogant, undisciplined, and even whimsical throughout 1 Kings 20:1–22. He assumes a palpable level of superiority vis-à-vis the nation of Israel and his royal counterpart. In addition, there are two interesting references to his alcohol consumption (20:12, 16), the second of which suggests that he likely entered the conflict in a state of inebriation: "Now Ben-Hadad was drinking himself drunk in the booths, with thirty-two kings helping him." Moreover, his drunkenness may have affected his tactics. Instead of seizing complete victory by means of neutralizing the entirety of the Israelite army, he perplexingly orders the capture of those coming out of Samaria (20:18).[2] Most

---

2. So DeVries: "Ben-Hadad is already scandalously drunk at noon. When the coming attack is reported to the bleary-eyed king, he seems more muddled than blood-thirsty, for the Israelites are to be taken alive whatever their intent" (Simon J. DeVries, 1 Kings, WBC 12, 2nd ed. [Dallas: Word, 2003], 249). Wray Beal appears less critical. She links the tactic of taking prisoners to a confidence in his coalition forces, all the while recognizing Ben-Hadad's arrogance and misperception of the situation (Wray Beal, 1 & 2 Kings, 265).

importantly, however, this characterization exists in stark contrast to the calm, matter of fact, and cogent disposition of the anonymous prophet of Yahweh.

Whereas Ben-Hadad's dictation of terms was inconsistent and confusing, the prophet's dictation was consistent and relatively simple (1 Kgs 20:13–14). The king of Israel was to appoint a small group of unproven administrators to lead the Israelite forces in open warfare against a large, seasoned coalition. The purpose of such an unconventional strategy, of course, was to ensure that Yahweh was credited for the victory.

> At that moment, a prophet approached Ahab, the king of Israel, and said, "Thus says Yahweh. You have seen all this great multitude. I am now delivering it today into your hand so that you may know that I am Yahweh." (1 Kgs 20:13)

But the clearest evidence that Ben-Hadad is being positioned against the anonymous prophet can be seen through their usage of the messenger formula *kōh ʾāmar* + name/title (name/title + כֹּה אָמַר).[3] The Aramean envoy prefaces their statements with *kōh ʾāmar ben-hădad* (כֹּה אָמַר בֶּן־הֲדַד), "thus says Ben-Hadad," which is contrasted with the prophetic use of *kōh ʾāmar YHWH* (כֹּה אָמַר יְהוָה), "thus says Yahweh."

The cumulative effect of this juxtaposition suggests that the Israelite king is positioned in this account between rival envoys jockeying for influence over Israel, creating the picture that Israel must yield to either a secular political entity or a divine one.[4] Furthermore,

---

3. The phrase *koh ʾāmar* (כֹּה אָמַר) appears 458 times in the Hebrew Bible, most notably in the corpus of prophetic literature. Within 1–2 Kings, the phrase occurs forty-four times. Of these, the name or title is YHWH or some derivation thereof, such as *YHWH ʾĕlohê yiśrāʾēl* (יְהוָה אֱלֹהֵי יִשְׂרָאֵל) in approximately 75% of the occurrences. Other names or titles in 1–2 Kings include *hammelek* (הַמֶּלֶךְ; "the king"; 1 Kgs 2:30; 22:37; 2 Kgs 1:11; 9:18; 18:29), *melek ʾaššûr* (מֶלֶךְ אַשּׁוּר; "the king of Assyria"; 2 Kgs 18:31), *hammelek haggāgôl melek ʾaššûr* (הַמֶּלֶךְ הַגָּדוֹל מֶלֶךְ אַשּׁוּר; "the great king, the king of Assyria"; 2 Kgs 18:19), *ḥizqîyāhû* (חִזְקִיָּהוּ; "Hezekiah"; 2 Kgs 19:3), and *ben-hădad* (2 Kgs 20:3, 5). Data retrieved via a phrase search "כֹּה אָמַר" in Logos Bible Software 9.

4. Hezekiah will later face a similar situation (Dominic Rudman, "Is the Rabshakeh also among the Prophets? A Rhetorical Study of 2 Kings XVIII 17–35," *VT* 50.1 [2000]: 100–110).

Israel's medial position informs the passive characterization of the Israelite king in this narrative. Terms are dictated to him, and the Israelite king appears to make decisions under pressure from both envoys. Even in audience with the elders, their words are volitional, suggesting notable influence upon the king: "All the elders and all the people said to him, 'Do not listen. Do not be willing'" (1 Kgs 20:8). The only place in this account where the Israelite king appears assertive is when he assembled the elders of Israel (20:7) and when he antagonized Ben-Hadad with his parable that one getting ready for battle should neither boast nor anticipate too much (20:11). But even in the case of the brash parable, it appears only after the Israelite king opens the door to reverting to the initial terms of capitulation. He is not proactive but rather reacts to the numerous dynamics of his crisis.

The king of Israel ultimately yields to the prophetic envoy against the Aramean one. He appoints what was likely a group of unproven leaders[5] over a force of 7,000 to depart Samaria and break the siege (20:14–15). Such strategy is significant. Leadership into battle by a group of unproven fighters against a seasoned coalition is shocking enough, but engagement in open field warfare would certainly expose their deficiencies. Yet in the end, the intentions of 1 Kings 20:13 are proven true. It is a "rout" (מַכָּה גְדוֹלָה, makkâ gədôlâ) in favor of the Israelites forces with the Israelite king pursuing the coalition forces (20:21). Nevertheless, Ben-Hadad escapes the carnage, poised to fight

---

5. The Hebrew phrase naʿărê śārê hammədînôt (נַעֲרֵי שָׂרֵי הַמְּדִינוֹת) has been subjected to substantial debate. On the one hand, Ramses II recounts the arrival of the Nearin-troops in preparation for his battle at Kadesh (ANET 256 n. 12), which many scholars follow while citing other comparative evidence (for a summary see Mordechai Cogan, I Kings: A New Translation with Introduction and Commentary, AB 10 [New Haven: Yale University Press, 2001], 464). However, Cogan is right when he says that the "tenor" of the account suggests a "more literal understanding" of naʿar (נַעַר), as "youth" or "young man." If the plural naʿărîm (נְעָרִים) is a group of elite troops, the glorification of Yahweh would be undermined. Van Wijk-Bos recognizes the possibility of both schools of thought, but remains non-committed, merely emphasizing that they appear as a type of "vanguard" (Johanna W. H. van Wijk-Bos, The Land and Its Kings: 1–2 Kings [Grand Rapids: Eerdmans, 2020], 143).

another day. This conclusion prepares the reader for the sequel that transpires the next spring.

Clearly, this account is presented in a sophisticated and artistic manner. Major players are characterized in light of others, and there is a palpable level of suspense and entertainment inherent in the presentation. Consequently, questions about the historical reliability of the account quickly rise to the surface. In particular, given the observable level of artistry involved with this account, to what degree does 1 Kings 20:1–22 reflect historical reality? To answer this, the remainder of the chapter will consider the historical relationship between Israel and Aram as well as the identity of Ben-Hadad alongside the identity of the Israelite king.

3.1 A HISTORY OF ISRAELITE/
ARAMEAN RELATIONS

Articulating a history between Aram and Israel is largely a one-sided affair. Except for the Tel Dan Stele and the Kurkh Monolith, the Old Testament is the only source that speaks directly to Aramean and Israelite relations. In light of this, it is paramount that specific statements in the Old Testament are evaluated in light of their overall context and historiographic intentions. This testimony is offered through two phases that are broadly chronological. The first phase describes Israelite and Aramean interaction during the patriarchal era of the Middle Bronze Age. Conversely, the second phase is more complex and overwhelmingly negative, appearing during the Iron Age, and showing no hint of positive relations. This is a significant departure from the Kurkh Monolith, which testifies to Israelite and Aramean cooperation against a shared foe.

3.1.1 THE PATRIARCHAL ERA—THE MIDDLE BRONZE AGE

It is prudent to begin with Deuteronomy as it explicitly claims distant kinship between Israel and the Arameans. Deuteronomy 26 recounts a firstfruits ceremony in which the pious Israelite was to take part. In

FIGURE 6: **The Kurkh Monolith Inscription, referencing the Battle of Qarqar and Ahab's role in the Syro-Palestinian coalition**

this ceremony, the Israelite was to take a sacrifice to a central sanctuary and make a specific confession before Yahweh.

> You will answer and say before Yahweh your God, "My father was a wandering[6] Aramean. He went down to Egypt, and he

---

6. The text is difficult, particularly since *ʾbd (אבד) can convey the sense of either "perish" or "stray" (*HALOT* 1:2). Moreover, both ideas of a "wandering Aramean" and an "ailing Aramean" display close connections with the patriarchal traditions. The patriarchs "wandered" to Egypt

sojourned there with a few people. He became there a great
and mighty nation with many people. And the Egyptians
treated us badly and oppressed us. They put upon us a hard
service. So we cried out to Yahweh, God of our fathers, and
Yahweh heard our voice and saw our affliction, our trouble,
and our oppression. So Yahweh brought us out from Egypt
with a strong hand, with an outstretched arm, with great awe,
with signs, and with wonders. He brought us to this place, and
he gave to us this land, a land flowing with milk and honey.
Consequently, I now have brought the first of the fruit of the
land, which you have given me, Yahweh." (Deut 26:5–10a)

The grammatical and text-critical discussions notwithstand-
ing, the clause *ʾărammî ʾōbēd ʾābî* (אֲרַמִּי אֹבֵד אָבִי), "my father was a
wandering Aramean," in 26:5 testifies that Israel and Aram shared
a common heritage, and that overlap is contextualized against the
Middle Bronze Age.[7] The referenced patriarch, "my father," whether
Abraham, Jacob, or the entirety of the patriarchal ancestors, is partially defined as Aramean. As a preparatory clause serving the more
salient issue of patriarchal migration to Egypt, the notation of distant Aramean kinship is dominated by the memory of the exodus,

---

because they were threatened by a lack of provision. Ultimately, it comes down to a choice
of preference. Craigie renders it "ailing" with an appeal to the "sense" of the passage (Peter
C. Craigie, *The Book of Deuteronomy*, NICOT [Grand Rapids: Eerdmans, 1976], 321 n. 4),
while Christensen translates it "wandering" because of the passage's "poetic quality" (Duane
L. Christensen, *Deuteronomy 21:10–34:12*, WBC 6B [Dallas: Word, 2002], 631). McConville
appeals to the emphasis upon the patriarchal sojourn to Egypt (J. G. McConville, *Deuteronomy*,
AOTC 5 [Downers Grove, IL: InterVarsity Press, 2002], 376), though the immediate context of
a firstfruits ceremony also lends credence to "starving" or "ailing." Moreover, Younger's note of
an Akkadian parallel (*arme ḫalqu munnabtu*), which results in "fugitive" or "refugee," is enticing
(Younger, *Political History of the Arameans*, 102–103).

7. On the grammatical and interpretive difficulties associated with this clause, see Richard
C. Steiner, "The 'Aramean' of Deuteronomy 26:5: Peshat and Derash," in *Telliah le-Moshe:
Biblical and Judaic Studies in Honor of Moshe Greenberg*, eds. M. Cogan, B. L. Eichler, and J. H.
Tigay (Winona Lake, IN: Eisenbrauns, 1997), 127–38; see also Younger, *Political History of the
Arameans*, 99–104.

suggesting that Israel's Aramean heritage exists only on the fringes of Israel's historical memory.[8]

A single referent behind the clause *'ărammî 'ōbēd 'ābî* is difficult to determine definitively as all three patriarchs and their families were associated with Aramean territories (e.g., Gen 24:10; 25:20; 28–31).[9] Nonetheless, this study accepts that Jacob is the most likely referent. Therefore, particular attention will be given to his history in Aramean territories. According to Genesis 28, he relocated to Paddan-aram in search for a suitable mate of non-Canaanite origin (28:1). Paddan-aram was also the home of his grandfather, Bethuel, and his mother, Rebekah (25:20; 28:2) and was likely located somewhere in northwestern Mesopotamia in the vicinity of Haran.[10] It was also the place where Jacob spent many years when he was coerced into service by the duplicity of his uncle Laban (Gen 29). Ultimately, after a long, profitable, but complicated relationship fraught with economic squabbles, Jacob left northwest Mesopotamia to migrate back to the southern Levant. However, Jacob's move did not happen until he secured a treaty with his Aramean relatives (31:43–55).

Consequently, Genesis remembers a complicated but profitable relationship with Aram. Jacob's life in Paddan-aram and his relationship with Laban were forged by deceptive mechanisms and characterized by tense interactions. Yet Jacob profited immensely in his foreign context (30:43).

---

8. The clause *'ărammî 'obēd 'ābîw* is a verbless clause, more specifically a declarative clause of identification (Bruce K. Waltke and Michael O'Connor, *An Introduction to Biblical Hebrew Syntax* [Winona Lake, IN: Eisenbrauns, 1990], §8.4). However, as John Cook has noted, the *wayyiqtol* form foregrounds the more salient information (John A. Cook, "The Semantics of Verbal Pragmatics: Clarifying the Roles of Wayyiqtol and Weqatal in Biblical Hebrew Prose," *Journal of Semitic Studies* 49.2 [2004]: 247–73). Thus, this independent clause prepares the reader for Jacob's migration to Egypt.

9. See page 52 n. 7.

10. The toponym Paddan-aram is only found in Genesis (25:20; 28:2, 5, 6, 7; 31:18; 33:18; 35:9, 26; 46:15). The precise location is difficult to pinpoint, due in large measure to its scarce attestation (always in association with Jacob's journeys) and the challenges associated with the meaning of *paddān* (see Wayne T. Pitard, "Paddan-Aram," *ABD* 5:55).

At this point, however, it seems useful to discuss the term "Aram" and "Aramean." Who were the Arameans, and whence did they come? How is it possible that Israel's heritage overlaps with Aramean heritage? How can one of ancient Israel's national confessions claim Aramean ancestry?

3.1.2 ON THE TERM ARAM AND ARAMEANS

The etymology of "Aram" (אֲרָם, 'ărām) is shrouded in uncertainty.[11] In the early twentieth century, a derivation from the root *rwm (רום) was proposed. This requires the presence of a prothetic aleph, a phonological phenomenon that is problematic but not without precedent.[12] Younger has pointed out the difficulties of such a proposal, not to mention the challenges of relating 'ărām to geographic, divine, and personal names.[13] Recently, Edward Lipinski argues for its relationship to the Arabic noun for "bull" or "buffalo," which is purportedly supported by religious iconography.[14] However, Younger questions the entire argument on linguistic grounds, concluding that "it is better to admit that this [etymology and meaning] still remains unknown."[15]

A bit clearer is the appearance of "Aram" in ancient Near Eastern texts. There is a possible appearance of "Aram" in an Egyptian toponym list dated to Amenhotep III and perhaps in a papyrus from the twelfth century. But these are heavily debated.[16] Without controversy are the occurrences of "Aram" in the annals of Tiglath-pileser I, who

---

11. We are indebted to Younger and Lipiniski for their summaries of the relevant data (Edward Lipinski, *The Arameans: Their Ancient History, Culture, Religion*, Orientalia Lovaniensia Analecta 100 [Leuven: Peeters, 2000], 51–54; Younger, *Political History of the Arameans*; 38–40).

12. Garr recognizes the possibility of prothetic *aleph* before sibilants in the initial position, but he also admits that the meager pool of data precludes the construction of a phonetic rule (W. Randall Garr, *Dialect Geography of Syria-Palestine: 1000–586 B.C.E* [Philadelphia: University of Pennsylvania Press, 1985; repr., Winona Lake, IN: Eisenbrauns, 2004], 47).

13. Younger, *Political History of the Arameans*, 38.

14. Lipinski, *Arameans*, 52–53.

15. Younger, *Political History of the Arameans*, 40.

16. For example, Görg argues for these references, but Lipinski argues against (M. Görg, "Aram und Israel," *VT* 26.4 [1976]: 499–500; Lipinski, *Arameans*, 32–33; see also Younger, *Political History of the Arameans*, 36 n. 4).

documents his ongoing conflicts with Aramean groups west of the Euphrates. As Younger points out, the Arameans were a constant problem.[17]

After Tiglath-pileser I, "Aram" increasingly appears across Akkadian literature, becoming one of the usual suspects in Akkadian royal literature. Interestingly, Akkadian texts do not refer to the Arameans of Aram-Damascus by the term "Aram" or "Aramean" but rather by the phrase "the House of Hazael" or by a pejorative associated with donkeys.[18] However, Aramaic sources do use the term "Aram" for polities associated with Damascus and Arpad.

Regardless of the nuances associated with scribal tendencies, it seems obvious that the increase of references to "Aram" or "Aramean" across the ancient Near Eastern textual record is indicative of the rising geopolitical significance of Aramean polities. While they were not strictly an Iron Age phenomenon, the range of occurrences of "Aram" and "Aramean" suggest that they were, for practical purposes, an Iron Age geopolitical reality. Whether in northwest Mesopotamia or further south in the Levant, the Arameans seized opportunities presented by the collapse of the Late Bronze Age to establish and expand their culture during the Iron Age. Thus, Younger is certainly correct in his reconstruction of the Arameans when he describes a sophisticated nomadic origin across three distinct regions in the context of the Late Bronze Age collapse.[19] And such a reconstruction, incidentally, establishes the Arameans as an interesting sociopolitical parallel to Israel.[20]

---

17. K. Lawson Younger Jr., "Tiglath-Pileser I and the Initial Conflicts of the Assyrians with the Arameans," in *Wandering Arameans: Arameans Outside Syria; Textual and Archaeological Perspectives*, ed. Angelika Berlejung, Aren M. Maeir, and Andreas Schüle (Wiesbaden: Harrassowitz Verlag, 2017), 195–228.

18. Younger, *Political History of the Arameans*, 550, 553.

19. Younger, *Political History of the Arameans*, 63–70.

20. At this point, we are speaking in general terms. Israel too, as a recognized polity, was forged in the aftermath of the Late Bronze Age collapse. Moreover, Israel's settlement in the central highland during the Iron Age was the result of a complex social development that involved military action, migration, and the amalgamation of indigenous groups (see Lawson G. Stone, "Early Israel and Its Appearance in Canaan," in *Ancient Israel's History: An Introduction*

At this point, we must return to the question regarding Israel's claim to Aramean heritage. It appears then that the Old Testament remembers that their heritage, specifically manifested in the exploits of the patriarchs, showed points of contact with regions that would later produce important Aramean polities. In the words of Younger, the memories of the Pentateuch are best understood as "functional anachronisms" used for practical communication when a "'right' [descriptor] might require many words with no assurance that there would be an intelligible communication."[21] The Pentateuchal writers used a reference that would have likely been familiar to their Iron Age audience. They were essentially communicating: "Our forefathers came from the regions that you now know to be Aramean territory. However, whatever Aramean identity they may have had, the experiences of the exodus—*our defining historical memory*—frames our memory."

3.1.3 THE PRE-MONARCHAL AND MONARCHAL ERAS—THE IRON AGE

During the Iron Age, Israelite/Aramean relations were marked by an increasing amount of hostility. According to the book of Judges, Yahweh sold (מכר, *mkr*) the Israelites into the service of Cushanrishathaim (כּוּשַׁן רִשְׁעָתַיִם, *kûšan rišʿātayim*) from Aram-naharaim (אֲרַם נַהֲרַיִם, *ʾăram nahărāyim*) for eight years (Judg 3:8), a turn of events that was interpreted as the direct consequence of Israel's apostasy. This servitude was eventually overturned by the heroic efforts of Othniel.

Particularly notable in this account is the general anonymity[22] of Israel's oppressor: "Cushan of Double-Wickedness of Aram of Two

---

to *Issues and Sources*, ed. Bill T. Arnold and Richard S. Hess [Grand Rapids: Baker Academic, 2014], 127–64).

21. Younger, *Political History of the Arameans*, 106. Younger is leaning on S. Nuccetelli, "Reference and Ethnic Groups," *Inquiry* 14 (2004): 1–17.

22. General anonymity refers to a textual tendency to use general references, like a title or office, with much greater frequency than specific identifiers like proper names. In this case,

Rivers." While in its literal sense this notation is essentially nonsensical, it can be clarified as "the Ethiopian King of Double Wickedness from Mesopotamia."[23] Yet even with this clarification, difficulties persist. First, there is a cross-pollination of ethnic terms—an Ethiopian king ruling an Aramean polity from Mesopotamia. Second, there are geographic and logistical difficulties—Israel's oppressor is associated with a territory positioned between the Tigris and the Euphrates. Perhaps Aram-naharaim is referring to a region between the Euphrates and one of its tributaries, which is not without precedent.[24] Perhaps the crossing of Cush with Aram is a literary device, as concluded by Stone: "The title is an alias serving the literary function of the story."[25] Most intriguing, however, is the realization that a similar convention of general anonymity is utilized more consistently in later Israelite recollections.

Aramean influence persisted throughout the period of the judges, in which their influence was observed in the apostate manifestations of Israelite religion (Judg 10:6) and the general politics of the northern regions of Israel (18:28). However, Israelite/Aramean relations were eventually expanded, intensified, and nationalized during the era of David. According to 2 Samuel 8:5–6, the Arameans of Damascus and Zobah suffered particularly because of David's ambitions—he set up garrisons in Damascus and imposed tribute. Of course, the rhetoric and precision of such claims should be analyzed critically.[26] Either way, David's ambition and charisma allowed Israel to gain the upper hand over the Aramean polities in his immediate vicinity. Almost certainly, such dominance was associated with the Aramean failures

---

the general anonymity refers to a specific person by means of their oppressive characteristics and general geographic origin.

23. Lawson G. Stone, "Judges," in *Joshua, Judges, Ruth*, Cornerstone Biblical Commentary (Carol Stream, IL: Tyndale House Publishers, 2012), 234.

24. Cundall cites this occasional tendency among Assyrian and Egyptian sources (Arthur Cundall, *Judges and Ruth: An Introduction and Commentary*, TOTC 7 [Downers Grove, IL: InterVarsity Press, 1968], 74).

25. Stone, "Judges," 234.

26. So Halpern, *David's Secret Demons*, 208–26.

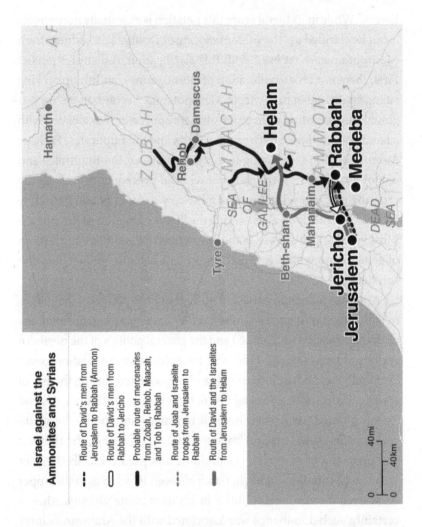

MAP 3: **Israel against the Ammonites and Syrians**

of their Ammonite coalition. Aramean soldiers were brought into the Israelite/Ammonite conflict that began when the Ammonite Hanun rebuffed and publicly shamed the Israelite envoy dispatched by David (2 Sam 10:1–2). Unfortunately for this Aramean force, Joab masterfully navigated the battle as well as the subsequent engagements to rout them and impose a treaty of peace (10:19).

Aramean influence upon the affairs of David's kingdom was also indirect. Absalom ostensibly gained sanctuary in Aramean territory during his exile, even uttering an oath of support in preparation for his return to Israelite society (2 Sam 15:8). Also, certain inhabitants of Abel Beth-Maacah, a locale in northern Israel connected to Aramean culture (see 10:6), handed over the corpse of Sheba after he revolted against David and thereby secured their lives during Joab's siege.[27] That Sheba sought sanctuary at Abel Beth Maacah—coupled with the reality that Absalom sought refuge in Aram Geshur—suggests that Aramean groups sought to disrupt Israelite political ambitions both overtly and covertly. It appears that anyone who opposed the policies of the Davidic administration could enjoy refuge in nearby Aramean territory.

This disruption of the Davidic administration continued into the reign of Solomon. Rezon, a political dissident of King Hadad-ezer of Zobah, gathered a group of disenfranchised individuals to form a faction of "raiders" (גְּדוּדִים, gədûdîm). The book of Kings contextualizes their founding and Rezon's authority over Damascus against the backdrop of Davidic aggression. Thus, Rezon and his group of dissidents function as Solomon's "adversary" (שָׂטָן, śāṭān; 1 Kgs 11:25) throughout his reign. Rezon's group apparently shared a deep disdain for Israel and David.

According to the extant textual record, Aramean and Israelite hostilities again rose during the Omride dynasty. The intense hostilities of the Omride and Jehuite dynasties eventually developed into Aramean and Judahite hostilities. Traditional Israelite/Aramean tensions would

---

27. According to 2 Samuel 10:6, soldiers from Abel Beth Maacah took part in the Aramean-Ammonite coalition. Similarly, the material culture at Abel Beth Maacah shows strong affinities with Aramean culture (see Naava Pantiz-Cohen and Robert A. Mullins, "Aram-Maacah? Arameans and Israelites on the Border: Excavations at Tell Abil el-Qamah (Abel-beth-maacah) in Northern Israel," in In Search for Aram and Israel: Politics, Culture, and Identity, ed. Omer Sergi, Manfred Oeming, and Izaak J. de Hulster [Tübingen: Mohr Seibeck, 2016], 139–68).

be set aside during the Syro-Ephriamite War (734–732 BC), reflecting the way those tensions were pacified for the battle of Qarqar (853 BC) and the subsequent advances of Shalmaneser III.[28] Similarly, Jeremiah testifies to Aramean and Babylonian cooperation during the siege of Jerusalem (Jer 35:11).

This brief survey of the biblical perspective reveals that Israelite and Aramean relations were extremely complex. Whatever heritage the two groups shared, the socio-political realities of the Iron Age eventually drove a wedge between the two cultures. This wedge would only be placed aside in the face of a common foe. Consequently, in the absence of any worthy cause, traditional rivalries were left to fester and develop into skirmishes and even full-blown conflicts. Moreover, it appears that the historic rivalry between Aram and Israel owed its development, at least in part, to similar socio-political realities. Both Israel and Aram were forged by comparable mechanisms during an overlapping era in the context of the Levant. Both cultures were the result of a multifaceted migration into territory left open by the Late Bronze Age collapse.[29]

From a historiographic standpoint, the biblical discussion of Israelite and Aramean relations displays an occasional, but interesting, capability for historiographic anonymity. The testimony of Judges is particularly informative here. Judges refers to a historic oppressor who, while described through imprecise notations, is associated with Aramean territories. The remainder of this chapter will begin to discuss how this mechanism of anonymity is observed again in the discussion of Omride and Aramean relations.

---

28. According to 2 Kings 15–16 and Isaiah 7, Rezin of Damascus cooperated with Pekah of Israel to coerce Ahaz and Judah into a coalition. Such coercion was important, for any Judean-Assyrian coalition would undermine the effectiveness of any Syro-Israelite coalition that had been forged in the wake of Assyria's advance.

29. For more on this collapse, see Cline, 1177 B.C., passim.

3.2 THE ANONYMITY OF BEN-HADAD IN 1 KINGS 20

In 1 Kings 20, the Aramean king is referred to as Ben-Hadad (בֶּן־הֲדַד, *ben hădad*, "son of Hadad"), a phrase that has proven to be quite difficult to narrow down to a specific person. At least three considerations have contributed to this difficulty. First, *ben hădad* appears many times in several different contexts across the Old Testament. First Kings 20 uses it extensively to refer to an otherwise unspecified Aramean king during the time of Ahab (20:1, 3, 5, 9, 10, 16, 17, 20, 26, 30, 32, 33). In contrast, one Ben-Hadad also appears during the reigns of Asa of Judah and Baasha of Israel (1 Kgs 15:18). This trend of using *ben hădad* to refer to various Aramean kings likewise continues in even later contexts (2 Kgs 6:24; 8:7–9; 13:3, 24–25). However, a few of these references specify the identity of *ben hădad* as "the son of Hazael" (בֶּן־חֲזָאֵל, *ben hăzāʾēl*; 2 Kgs 13:3, 24–25). There are also places outside of Kings where *ben hădad* appears (Jer 49:27; Amos 1:4; 2 Chr 16:2–4).[30] Consequently, if *ben hădad* is a proper name, then the chronology behind all these occurrences suggests at least two Aramean kings with the same name, perhaps even three. Thus, biblical scholars often refer to a Ben-Hadad I, a Ben-Hadad II, and potentially a Ben-Hadad III.

Second, presuming that *ben hădad* is a proper name results in linguistic incompatibility between the biblical naming vis-à-vis the parallel naming in other historical records. The Assyrian account of the battle of Qarqar mentions that Ahab reigned alongside the Aramean Adad-idri, known as *hădadʿezer* (Hadad-ezer) in the biblical corpus (1 Kgs 20). However, the appellation *ben hădad* is not linguistically compatible with *hădadʿezer*.[31] Some have proposed that Hadad-ezer and Ben-Hadad are two names referring to the same person, akin to Jehoahaz/Ahaziah and the various spellings of Jehoiachin/Jeconiah/

---

30. In Amos 1:4, *ben hădad* is in a parallel relationship with *bêt hăzāʾēl* (בֵּית־חֲזָאֵל).
31. Most notably, Younger, *Political History of the Arameans*, 581.

Coniah.[32] However, Younger has astutely noticed that in the cases invoked as support for this analogy, the biblical examples boil down to transposing consonants.[33] In comparison, there is significant discontinuity between Hadad-ezer and Ben-Hadad.

The final difficulty associated with *ben hădad* arises from its meaning, "son of Hadad." Donald J. Wiseman popularized the theory that *ben hădad* referred not to a proper name but rather to a generalized dynastic title, although this proposal is not without issues.[34] The Zakkur Inscription aligns with 2 Kings 13 when it refers to Hazael's son as "Bar-Hadad," the Aramaic equivalent to "Ben-Hadad." Similarly, the Melqart Stele references one "Bir-Hadad son of Attarhamek," who commissioned the monument in response to Melqart's favor.[35] Consequently, it seems that the biblical tendency to use a generalized dynastic title is mirrored in other inscriptions. Using a dynastic title forces the acceptance of a certain level of historiographic imprecision. Why generalize the reference to Aramean kings, and in the Bible's case, why do it so often?

In our estimation, Younger has offered the definitive statement in response to the current data.[36] According to Younger, the Assyrian nuances are critical. The Assyrians referred to Aramean kings by their personal names, whereas "the son of Hadad" (through Ben-Hadad and Bar-Hadad) is a phenomenon unique to a few voices among West Semitic materials. Younger concludes:

---

32. For example, Iain Provan, V. Philips Long, and Tremper Longman III, *A Biblical History of Israel* (Louisville: Westminster John Knox, 2003), 369 n. 30.

33. Younger, *Political History of the Arameans*, 581–82 n. 123.

34. Donald J. Wiseman, *1 and 2 Kings*, TOTC 9 (1993; repr., Downers Grove, IL: IVP Academic, 2008), 188. See Benjamin Mazar's earlier proposal that the Ben-Hadad of 1 Kings 20 was "none other than Adad-idri (Hadadezer)" (Benjamin Mazar, "The Aramean Empire and Its Relations with Israel," *BA* 25 [1962]: 106).

35. The Melqart Stele has proven to be controversial, particularly with respect to the region over which Bir-Hadad rules ("The Melqart Stele," translated by Wayne Pitard [*COS* 2.33:152–153]).

36. See Younger, *Political History of the Arameans*, 583–84.

While theoretically it is entirely possible that Bar-Hadad (Ben-Hadad) was a personal name, there is actually very little evidence for it. Consequently, it seems very possible that Bar-Hadad (Ben-Hadad) was a dynastic name, perhaps based on a personal name, similar to Hittite "Larbarna," Latin "Caesar," or a dynastic title like Egyptian "Pharoah" ("Great House"), etc.[37]

That *ben hădad* is neither a personal name nor a specific reference aligns this anonymity with other observed anonymities throughout 1 Kings 20:1–22. The prophet who functions as a foil to Ben-Hadad is merely described as "a certain prophet" (נָבִיא אֶחָד, *nābî' 'eḥad*), and there is the general reference to the "junior governors of the province" (*naʿarê śārê hamməđînôt*).[38] In addition, there is an overwhelming preference for "the king of Israel" (מֶלֶךְ יִשְׂרָאֵל, *melek yiśrā'ēl*), rather than the king's personal name.

TABLE 3: The occurrences of *melek yiśrā'ēl* and Ahab in 1 Kings 20

melek yiśrā'ēl	Ahab
1 Kgs 20:2, 4, 7, 11, 13, 21, 22, 28, 31, 32, 40, 41, 43	1 Kgs 20:2, 13, 14

Indeed, of Ahab's three mentions, one is textually suspect, resulting in only two occurrences.[39] The overwhelming preference for "the

---

37. Younger, *Political History of the Arameans*, 584. In our minds, the biblical tendency to refer overwhelmingly to the Egyptian king as "Pharoah" or "king of Egypt" is a striking parallel. Apparently, only certain situations facilitated the need to reference the foreign king by a specific name.

38. For a discussion of this phrase, see David B. Schreiner, "Breaking the Siege: Examining the נַעֲרֵי שָׂרֵי הַמְּדִינוֹת in 1 Kgs 20," *The Asbury Journal* 77.2 (2002): 378–99.

39. The textual tradition of 1 Kings 20:13 shows that *'aḥ'āb* (אַחְאָב; "Ahab") does not appear in Codex Vaticanus, the Lucianic recension, or in Waltonii's edition of the Peshitta. The problems with Waltonii's edition are widely known, though Vaticanus is a formidable witness. DeVries accepts the variant, calling the MT's usage of *'aḥ'āb* "explicative" (DeVries, 1 *Kings*, 244). Wray Beal (1 & 2 *Kings*, 260) and Cogan (I *Kings*, 460) retain the MT but offer no explanation. In any respect, whether *'aḥ'āb* appears twice or three times in 1 Kings 20, the point remains that the historian's tendency is to emphasize the institution and de-emphasize the individual.

king of Israel" coupled with the other anonymous features emphasizes
social institutions while de-emphasizing specific people.[40]

3.3 ANONYMITY AS A LITERARY CONVENTION?

The prevailing tendency to use *melek* (מֶלֶךְ, "king") and the construct
chain *melek yiśrā'ēl* ("king of Israel") has been demonstrated at a general level. Is this tendency indicative of a larger trend?

The noun *melek* appears 1,104 times in the Deuteronomistic
History as a singular noun, and 113 times as a plural noun.[41] Within
the books of 1–2 Kings, *melek* appears 603 times in the singular and 72
times in the plural. With the definite article, the occurrences of *melek*
(הַמֶּלֶךְ, *hammelek*) shrink to 549 times in the Deuteronomistic History
and to 268 times in Kings. The definite plural form *hammǝlākîm*
(הַמְּלָכִים) appears only 31 times in the Deuteronomistic History and 8
times in Kings. The combined occurrences of the singular and plural
construct forms of *melek* tally 463, and in Kings the number comes
to 325.[42] With one exception in 1 Kings 20:31, all the construct forms
in Kings appear with some type of geopolitical notation in the construct chain's absolute position. In 20:1–43, *melek* appears 10 times in
the absolute state, and 14 times in construct with *yiśrā'ēl*.

This data is important because it has been invoked as evidence
for redactional activity. Beginning in the middle of the twentieth century scholars have pointed out the awkwardness of 1 Kings 20 and 22.
Literarily, virtually every scholar notes the relatively sparse identification of Ahab alongside the prominence of the phrase *melek yiśrā'ēl*.[43]

---

40. Mark A. Leucther and David T. Lamb, *The Historical Writings: Introducing Israel's Historical Literature* (Minneapolis: Fortress, 2016), 283.

41. Data compiled from Logos Bible Software 9, searching "lemma:1:מֶלֶךְ@N??S and lem-ma:1:מֶלֶךְ@N??P" in *Biblia Hebraica Stuttgartensia: SESB 2.0 Version*, electronic ed. (Stuttgart: Deutsche Bibelgesellschaft, 2003).

42. Data compiled from Logos Bible Software 9, searching "lemma:1:מֶלֶךְ@N???C" in *Biblia Hebraica Stuttgartensia: SESB 2.0 Version*.

43. As a reminder, in 1 Kings 20, the title *melek yiśrā'ēl* appears thirteen times, while the name of said king only appears two or three times (or two; see note 39 above). Furthermore,

TABLE 4: Occurrences of *melek* in the Deuteronomistic History (DtrH)

Form	Inflection	Occurrences in Kings	Occurrences in DtrH
melek	masc., sing., abs.	603	1,104
melakim	masc., pl., abs.	72	113
hammelek	masc., sing. abs., def.	268	549
hamməlākîm	masc., pl., abs., def.	8	31
melek	masc., sing., constr.	325	463
malkê	masc., pl., constr.		

As a result, various royal candidates have been put forward as refer-
ents because their context seems to better fit the Aramean war narrative, namely, the lopsided superiority of the Arameans. Among the
likely candidates are Joram (DeVries), Jehoahaz (Steven McKenzie,
J. Maxwell Miller), and Joash (A. Jepsen, McKenzie, Wayne Pitard,
C. F. Whitley, Marsha White).[44] According to these views, the intru-
sion of Ahab's name in 1 Kings 20 is explained as an editorial gloss,
thereby "underscoring the failure of the Omride kings" by associ-
ating the king of Israel with Ahab explicitly.[45] As summed up by
McKenzie: "The paucity and irregularity of occurrences of Ahab's
name suggests that his identification as the king of Israel in these
stories is secondary."[46] But such a position forces a larger discussion.

---

in 1 Kings 22:1–40 (ending with the death of Ahab), the king's name appears three times (1 Kgs
22:20, 39, 40), two of which appear in the Deuteronomistic formulaic conclusion to the king's
reign. By contrast, *melek yiśrāʾēl* appears seventeen times in the same narrative.

44. DeVries, 1 *Kings*, 269; J. Maxwell Miller, "The Fall of the House of Ahab," *VT* 17.3 (1967):
307–24; Steven L. McKenzie, *The Trouble with Kings: The Composition of the Book of Kings in
the Deuteronomistic History*, Supplements to Vetus Testamentum 42 (Leiden: Brill, 1991), 90; A.
Jepsen, "Israel und Damascus," *Archiv für Orientforschung* 14 (1942): 154–59; McKenzie, *Trouble
with Kings*, 90; Wayne Pitard, *Ancient Damascus: A Historical Study of the Syrian City-State from
Earliest Times until Its Fall to the Assyrians in 732 B.C.E.* (Winona Lake, IN: Eisenbrauns, 1987),
115–25; Marsha White, "Naboth's Vineyard and Jehu's Coup: The Legitimation of a Dynastic
Extermination," *VT* 44.1 (1994): 66–76; C. F. Whitley, "The Deuteronomic Presentation of
the House of Omri," *VT* 2.2 (1952): 137–52.

45. De Vries, 1 *Kings*, 270.

46. McKenzie, *Trouble with Kings*, 89–90.

If Ahab is secondary to 1 Kings 20, and chapter 22 for that matter, one must account for his secondary association through appeals to a redactor or editor. In other words, advocates of Ahab's secondary status in these chapters are also advocates of a complicated redactional program.[47]

However, this relative lack of naming Ahab vis-à-vis the predominance of "the king of Israel" can be understood differently. David Lamb argues that displacing these narratives from their current context in the Masoretic Text remains unconvincing.[48] While Ahab's name is relatively sparse throughout chapters 20 and 22, it appears extensively in 1 Kings 21. The two contexts are tied together with the repeated hendiadys "sullenly vexed" (סַר וְזָעֵף, sar wəzāʿēp; 1 Kgs 20:43; 21:4).[49] More interesting is the explicit reference to Jehoshaphat throughout 1 Kings 22. As pointed out by Lamb, to argue that these narratives were original to another context requires that one also explain the presence of Jehoshaphat, an Omride contemporary in Judah.[50] Finally, as Lamb points out, suggestions that the geopolitical situation described in the Omride wars depicted in 1 Kings 20, 22, and 2 Kings 3 does not comport with extrabiblical descriptions can be explained by the propagandistic function of the extrabiblical witnesses.

In the vein of Lamb's arguments against large scale redactional reworking, there is evidence to suggest that the usage of *melek* and

---

47. For a concise summary of the issues, see McKenzie, *Trouble with Kings*, 88–93. See also the important arguments of J. Maxwell Miller, "The Elisha Cycle and the Accounts of the Omride Wars," *JBL* 85 (1966): 441–54; Shuichi Hasegawa, "Looking for Aphek in 1 Kings 20," *VT* 62 (2012): esp. 504–10.

48. David T. Lamb, *Righteous Jehu and His Evil Heirs: The Deuteronomist's Negative Perspective on Dynastic Succession* (Oxford: Oxford University Press, 2008), 200–204.

49. Lamb, *Righteous Jehu*, 202. Lamb admits that it is possible that this hendiadys is redactional, "to make a smooth seam," but he suggests that it would have been easier to just add Ahab to chapter 20. Nevertheless, the ancient textual witness regarding the sequence of 1 Kings 20–22 is complicated. For example, the Septuagint places its translation of chapter 21 (3 Kingdoms 20) immediately before its translation of chapters 20 and 22 (3 Kingdoms 21–22).

50. This often forces the expansion of an already elaborate redactional program. For example, McKenzie argues that Jehoshaphat was included in the originally anonymous tradition of 1 Kings 22 "on the basis of 2 Kings 3" (McKenzie, *Trouble with Kings*, 92).

melek yiśrā'ēl may be indicative of a specific historiographic convention. Upon surveying the occurrences of *melek* in the historiographic literature ideologically related to 1–2 Kings—namely, the so-called Deuteronomistic History—three categories emerge.

- **Identifiable King**: a king may be readily identified by the immediate context and is mentioned with a relatively high frequency within the pericope.

- **Generally Anonymous King**: a king is named, but the prevailing tendency is to refer to the king by a generic title, or the king is not named specifically and remains anonymous throughout the pericope, but his identity is clarified by its surrounding context.

- **Unmistakably Anonymous King**: a king is not named or identifiable by context and is referred to as *hammelek* or "the king of [geographical place name]."

Interestingly, each of these categories can be observed in Joshua 10. Table 5 clarifies the categories and their appearance in that chapter.

Of particular interest for this study is the category "Generally Anonymous King," an observable phenomenon in many locations across the Deuteronomistic History.

3.3.1 EVIDENCE FROM THE DEUTERONOMISTIC HISTORY

1 Samuel 12

Throughout the entire chapter of 1 Samuel 12, Saul is never mentioned by name. However, in 1 Samuel 11 he is mentioned by name nine times and an additional fifteen times in 1 Samuel 13. First Samuel 12 begins with a reminder that the prophet Samuel "set a king over" the Israelites. This king is then referred to as *hammelek* five times in the following fourteen verses (1 Sam 12:2, 13, 14).

TABLE 5: Categories of anonymity in Joshua 10

Passage	Category	Commentary
Josh 10:33 "Then Horam king of Gezer went up to assist Lachish, so Joshua struck down him and his people. There were no survivors."	Identifiable King	The king of Gezer appears on the scene, and he and his army are struck down. He is never again referred to as *hammelek* or *melek gezer*.
Josh 10:3 "So Adoni-zedek king of Jerusalem notified Hoham king of Hebron, Piram king of Jarmuth, Japhia king of Lachish, and Debir king of Eglon."	Generally Anonymous King	Subsequent to 10:3, the kings are mentioned again as "the five Amorite kings" (10:5), "the five kings" (10:17), and "these five kings" (10:16, 22–23). Of these, Hoham and Piram never appear again in the biblical record. Both Japhia (Josh 19:12) and Debir (Judg 1:11) appear as geographical place names (Josh 19:12; Judg 1:11), but neither are mentioned again as kings in the biblical corpus. Adoni-zedek appears in one other place (Josh 10:1). In short, each of these five kings are referenced five times in a pericope that encompasses twenty-seven verses, but they are only identified by name once, with the exception of Adoni-zedek.
Josh 10:28 "That day Joshua captured Makkedah and defeated it by the edge of the sword, utterly destroying[51] them and their king; he left no survivors. So he did to the king of Makkedah exactly what he had done to the king of Jericho."	Unmistakably Anonymous King	The king of Makkedah is never identified by name, though he also appears in the list of thirty-one kings Joshua defeated west of the Jordan (Josh 12:16).

---

51. On the elusive meaning and broad semantics of *ḥerem*, see our discussion in chapter 4.

1 Samuel 22

In the account of Saul's encounter with the priests at Nob (1 Sam 22:6–23), the narrative begins with explicit reference to Saul. He is identified by name six times in 22:6–13. In the next eight verses (22:14–19) in which Saul converses with Ahimelech, Saul's name does not appear, whereas *hammelek* appears eight times. Saul resurfaces twice in the final three verses of the chapter. Thus, Saul is mentioned eight times in 22:6–23, but at the center of the pericope his name is replaced by the anonymous *hammelek*.

2 Samuel 14

When Absalom returned to Jerusalem after killing Amnon and fleeing the city (2 Sam 14), David's name is completely absent from the text while *hammelek* appears thirty-five times. In contrast, David appears four times in 2 Samuel 13 and eight times in 2 Samuel 15.

2 Samuel 18–19

Second Samuel 18–19 recounts the death of Absalom and its subsequent aftermath including David's dealings with Shimei, Mephibosheth, and Barzillai. Within these two chapters—a total of seventy-six verses—David is identified as *hammelek* eighty-four times while his personal name appears a mere nine times. On two occasions, the text refers to "David the king" (19:11, 16).

2 Kings 3

In J(eh)oram's battle with Moab, narrated in 2 Kings 3:4–27, the phrase *melek yiśrāʾēl* occurs eight times. Moreover, *melek môʾāb* ("king of Moab") appears three times (3:4, 5, 7) and *melek yəhûdâ* ("king of Judah") appears once (3:9). The king of each is identified by name at least once: Mesha, the king of Moab (3:4); J(eh)oram, the king of Israel (3:6); and Jehoshaphat, the king of Judah (3:7, 11, 12, 14).

2 Kings 5:1–8:15

At the heart of the Elisha Cycle, these chapters are dedicated to miracles in a royal context, namely the healing of the Aramean military officer Naaman and the Aramean siege of Samaria. In the entirety of these ninety-five verses Ben-Hadad is identified by name three times (2 Kgs 6:24; 8:7, 9) and Hazael five times (2 Kgs 8:8, 9, 12, 13), while *melek ʾărām* ("king of Aram") occurs seven times (2 Kgs 5:1, 5; 6:8, 11, 24; 8:7, 9).[52] By contrast, Israel's king J(eh)oram remains completely anonymous within this pericope, while *melek yiśrāʾēl* appears eleven times and *hammelek* occurs an additional nineteen times, always in reference to Israel's king.[53]

2 Kings 11

The final example of anonymous Israelite and Judahite kings germane to this conversation appears in 2 Kings 11, which depicts Athaliah's violent takeover of Judah. Athaliah's son Ahaziah, who had died in Megiddo at the hands of Jehu's archers (9:27), is referenced twenty times in 2 Kings 11 as *hammelek*. His name appears in 11:1 as the son of Athaliah, and twice in 11:2 as the brother or Jehosheba and the father of Joash.

In addition to these examples of Generally Anonymous Kings of Israel and Judah, there are two prominent Old Testament examples of Generally Anonymous Kings who are non-Israelite and non-Judahite.

2 Kings 17–20

In 2 Kings 17–18, Shalmaneser V is credited with defeating Samaria (17:3; 18:9), while Sennacherib is credited with capturing Judah's military outposts (18:13) and besieging Jerusalem during Hezekiah's reign (19:16, 20, 36). Despite the relative clarity regarding their identity, the historian overwhelmingly uses the anonymous moniker *melek aššûr*

---

52. On the use of Ben-Hadad in 2 Kings and extrabiblical sources, see chapter 4.

53. For the eleven occurrences of *melek yiśrāʾēl*, see 2 Kings 5:5, 6, 7, 8; 6:9, 10, 11, 12, 21, 26; 7:6. For the nineteen occurrences of *hammelek*, see 2 Kings 5:8; 6:12, 26, 28, 30; 7:9, 11, 12, 14, 17 (2x), 18; 8:3, 4, 5 (2x), 6 (2x), 8.

("king of Assyria"), which might be explained by the obscurity associated with the actual capture of Samaria.[54]

2 Kings 25

Within the account of Jerusalem's fall to Babylon, Nebuchadnezzar is identified six times (2 Kgs 24:1, 10–11; 25:1, 8, 22), while he is referred to as *melek bābel* ("king of Babylon") eight more times.[55] Both the literary context and the historical record are unambiguous with respect to his identity.

In summary, this survey has displayed a tendency within the historiographic literature related to Kings to make extensive reference to specific kings through generic means. Critical for each instance is an awareness of the larger literary context as it often clarifies, albeit through diverse methods, the anonymity. The Assyrian and Babylonian Chronicles provide another point of comparison.[56]

3.3.2 EVIDENCE FROM MESOPOTAMIAN CHRONICLES

Although the Deuteronomistic History and the Assyrian and Babylonian Chronicles have their own distinct ideological agendas, they both recount the deeds of their royalty. Similarly, these chronicles also employ the category Generally Anonymous King, though none of these twenty-one texts present a king as Unmistakably Anonymous.

---

54. Across 2 Kings 17–19, the occurrences are: 17:4–6 (5 times), 24–27 (3 times); 18:7, 11, 14 (2 times), 16–17 (2 times), 19, 23, 28, 30–31 (2 times), 33; 19:4, 6, 8, 10–11 (2 times), 17, 32. Interestingly, the Assyrian annals credit both Shalmaneser V and Sargon II for the sacking of Samaria. Shalmaneser V died in 722, the year he imprisoned Hoshea for treachery against Assyria by seeking assistance from Egypt. His half-brother usurped the throne and took the name *Sharru-kenu* ("true king"), better known as Sargon II, who incidentally took credit for the sacking of Samaria. This is not the context to engage this historical question, although it's clear that both Shalmaneser V and Sennacherib were the Assyrian kings during the reign of Hezekiah. For a summary of the debate and possible ways to interpret it, see Josette Elayi, *Sargon II: King of Assyria* (Atlanta: SBL Press, 2017), 48–50. See also Sarah C. Melville, "Sargon II," in *The Ancient Near East: Historical Sources in Translation*, ed. Mark W. Chavalas (Oxford: Blackwell, 2006), 333–42.

55. 2 Kings 24:12 (2 times), 16–17 (2 times), 20; 25:6, 8, 11, 20–21 (2 times), 23–24 (2 times).

56. A. K. Grayson, *Assyrian and Babylonian Chronicles* (Winona Lake, IN: Eisenbrauns, 2000).

Several texts, such as Chronicle 1, readily identify kings. There are numerous cases in which the kings are Generally Anonymous—three are discussed here as exemplars.

Chronicle 3, Fall of Nineveh Chronicle

Chronicle 3 is comprised of seventy-eight lines of cuneiform text and recounts regnal years 10–18 of Nabopolassar of Babylon.[57] The text records the fall of Nineveh to the Babylonians in year fourteen of his reign. Within these seventy-eight lines, Nabopolassar is identified by name only twice. Line 1 reads, "the tenth year of Nabopolassar." At each of the other year-date lines the king's name is omitted (e.g., "the eleventh year," "the twelfth year," etc.). The second occurrence of Nabopolassar's name is in line 3: "In the month of Ab the army of Assyria prepared for battle in Gablini and Nabopolassar went up against them." Throughout the remainder of Chronicle 3 the Babylonian king is simply referred to as "king of Akkad" (*šàr Akkadî*) thirty-two times.[58] The Assyrian king, Šin-šarru-iškun, is similarly identified by name only once, at the mention of his death. The other six references to this king are as "king of Assyria" (*šàr* ^kur^*Aššur*).

Chronicle 4, Chronicle concerning the Later Years of Nabopolassar

Chronicle 4 consists of twenty-eight lines of well-preserved cuneiform text and recounts regnal years 18–21 of Nabopolassar, the final years of his rule, in which he was turned back by Egyptian forces at Qurumatu.[59] In this chronicle, Nabopolassar is identified only in line 1 in the year-date formula. As with Chronicle 3, all other year-date formulae in the text lack the king's name. Thus, consecutive years are simply rendered "the nth year," where n represents the

---

57. Grayson, *Assyrian and Babylonian Chronicles*, 90–96.

58. Two of these instances occur within broken text reconstructed by Grayson. Whether Grayson's reconstructions of [*šàr A*]*kkadî* (line 28) and [*šàr Akkad*]*î* (line 29) are correct (and there is no other reasonable emendation), there is no room for *Nabû-àpla-úṣur* (Grayson, *Assyrian and Babylonian Chronicles*, 93).

59. Grayson, *Assyrian and Babylonian Chronicles*, 97–98.

regnal year. Throughout the remainder of the text Nabopolassar is called "king of Akkad" (šàr Akkadî) ten times. His eventual successor, Nebuchadnezzar, is mentioned by name twice (lines 6 and 27) and is not referenced elsewhere in the text.

Chronicle 7, Nabonidus Chronicle

Chronicle 7, known as the Nabonidus Chronicle, depicts the twilight and fall of darkness on the Neo-Babylonian Empire under the rule of Nabonidus.[60] This twenty-eight-line text presents a situation much like 2 Samuel 14, in which the king is identified at the peripheries, but remains anonymous for a large segment within the text. In this case, Nabonidus is identified once at year 9 and three times in year 17. Between years 9 and 17, however, this Babylonian king is identified simply as "king" (šarru) seven times with no mention of his name.[61]

3.4 CONCLUSIONS

Many scholars have interpreted the sporadic references to Ahab alongside the preference for the generic "king" or "king of Israel" as evidence for redactional activity in 1 Kings 20, 22, and elsewhere in the narratives associated with the Elijah and Elisha cycles. The text-critical situation of 1 Kings 20–22—namely, that major literary traditions (Masoretic vs. the Septuagintal traditions) exhibit a different ordering of the chapters—places the reality of redactional activity beyond question. But to build such complex redactional schemes on the general anonymity of the king of Israel ultimately suggests that similar arguments should likewise be applied to other historiographic contexts where this phenomenon also appears.

In contrast to the impetus for complicated redactional reconstructions, we propose that the observed degrees of anonymity are better understood as a historiographic literary convention. In some

---

60. Grayson, *Assyrian and Babylonian Chronicles*, 104–11.

61. It must be noted that much of the tablet for regnal years 1–5 is broken beyond recognition, so some caution must be exercised with making too bold of assertions with this text.

instances of our Unmistakably Anonymous Kings they illustrate a
fallen kingdom, such as the king of Jericho (Josh 2, 10), the king of Ai
(Josh 8), and the king of Makkedah (Josh 10).[62] It is also possible that
the identity of the king may simply be unknown to the historiographer
or unimportant for the narrative. Either of these might be behind the
anonymity of the king of Egypt until Shishak appears (1 Kgs 14:25),
or behind the anonymous king of Edom (2 Kgs 3:9, 12, 26). This
situation seems particularly plausible in the case of Chronicle 25 of
the Assyrian and Babylonian Chronicles in which the king of Mari,
a "son of a nobody" (*mār lā mamman*), was deposed by the Kassite
ruler Adad-šuma-uṣur.[63]

Regarding the Generally Anonymous Kings, the narrator, even
though the king's identity is obvious from context, intentionally renders the king as insignificant. Indeed, it is notoriously difficult to
determine intent, but perhaps a deliberate insignificance is behind
the references to the kings of Assyria, Babylon, and Egypt in the latter
chapters of 2 Kings. The names of the kings are important enough
to be mentioned several times, but not as important as the empires
they represent. There do not seem to be any examples of this type of
rhetoric from the Assyrian and Babylonian Chronicles.

In other instances, the king is rendered significant by virtue of the
repeated references to the office with little or no reference to the king's
name. Yet the king's status as king is more relevant to the narrator
than the name of the king. This seems to be the case especially in the
Assyrian and Babylonian Chronicles, in which the king is identified
by name minimally but is referred to as "king of Akkad" (*šàr Akkadî*)
throughout. In these instances, the kings seem to be making claims of
legitimization as the rightful heir to the throne in Babylon, connecting
their kingship to the royal line of Sargon. A biblical example is found

---

62. Most likely candidates for this category are kings of Jericho (Josh 2, 10), Ai (Josh
8), Makkedah (Josh 10), Shimron (Josh 11), Achshapsh (Josh 11), Ammon (Judge 11), Moab
(1 Sam 12), Hamath (2 Kgs 19), Arpad (2 Kgs 19), Sepharvaim (2 Kgs 19), Hena (2 Kgs 19),
and Ivva (2 Kgs 19).

63. On the characterization of a "son of nobody," see page 41 n. 78.

in 1 Samuel 22:6–23 in which the priest Ahimelech consistently refers to Saul as *hammelek*, while the narrator frequently refers to him by name. Presumably this narrative strategy demonstrates the priest's loyalty to the office. Another example might be 2 Samuel 14, where the narrator refers to David only as *hammelek*, perhaps in preparation for the coming usurpation by Absalom. By highlighting David's status as king, the narrator elevates the shock level of Absalom's play for the throne.

Finally, the anonymity of the king may, in fact, be due to the insertion of external source material. Candidates for this category might include 1 Kings 3:16–28, the case of the two prostitutes and the dead infant, and 2 Kings 4–8 from the Elisha Cycle. There are no such examples from the Assyrian and Babylonian Chronicles.

Specifically applied to 1 Kings 20 and 22, this general anonymity centering on King Ahab functions as a historiographic device informing a larger trend of anonymization. Ben-Hadad likewise reflects a generic reference to an Aramean king, the prophet of Yahweh is anonymous, the critical faction within the Israelite army were generically described as "the junior governors of the provinces" (*naʿarê śārê hammədînôt*), and the situations surrounding the battle were never explicitly declared. As we will see in the subsequent chapters, this trend will continue.

Chapter 4

THE BATTLE OF APHEK

The sequel to the siege of Samaria begins at 1 Kings 20:23. Interestingly, not all English translations note the transition in the same way. For example, the NRSV marks the passage with a paragraph heading, an editorial decision that notes the significance of the initial disjunctive clause: "Now the servants of the king of Aram said to him" (וְעַבְדֵי מֶלֶךְ־אֲרָם אָמְרוּ אֵלָיו, *wəʿabdê melek ʾărām āmərû ʾēlāyw*). However, the NIV softens any narratival shift, contextualizing 20:23 contemporaneously with 20:22. It translates the initial disjunctive clause with "meanwhile," although the grammar is ambiguous. Thus, it is quite possible to see the Aramean review of the siege of Samaria to be something that took place shortly after the Aramean defeat. Ultimately, however, the shift signified by the initial disjunctive clause in 20:23, the shift in topic, and the function of 20:23–25 as preparation for what follows in 20:26–34 are decisive in our minds.[1] Consequently, we understand 20:23 to start a new section in the recounting of the Omride and Aramean relationship.

---

1. Arnold and Choi highlight two reasons for altering the customary Hebrew verb-subject word order: emphasis on the subject and the change of subject. In this case, the second appears to be particularly appropriate (Bill T. Arnold and John H. Choi, *A Guide to Biblical Hebrew Syntax*, 2nd. ed [Cambridge: Cambridge University Press, 2018], 182–83).

What is unequivocal, however, is Ben-Hadad's singular focus to redeem the shocking upset of the previous season. During his siege of Samaria (1 Kgs 20:23–25) his military strategy has its genesis with his servants, not with his own creative imagination. According to 20:23, they build off the assumption that Israel's "gods are gods of the hills." Consequently, in their minds, the previous defeat makes perfect sense, for Aram erroneously engaged the Israelite army in their own territory, the central highlands, where "they prevailed against us."[2] In turn, the servants confidently propose that if the theater of war can be adjusted in their favor, then victory must logically follow: "Perhaps if we fight against them on the plain,[3] we will surely prevail over them." Unfortunately for the Aramean advisors, their logic, which appears so precise and is wielded with such confidence, will prove to be fallacious.

The Aramean advisors also seek to mirror the Israelite strategy that featured the na'ărê śārê hammədînôt, "the junior governors of the provinces" (1 Kgs 20:19), during the siege of Samaria. They replace the previously utilized "kings" (hamməlākîm) with a regiment of generically defined "officers" (פֶּחָה, peḥâ). While peḥâ is difficult to define precisely, it appears that these officers could implement unconventional warfare tactics.[4] Regardless of their abilities, the appointment of the peḥâ in place of hamməlākîm signals a deliberate change in their methods of engagement. But this is not to say that the Aramean force was less numerous. First Kings 20:25 makes it clear that the advisors' proposal included "an army like the army that fell from you—horse

---

2. This logic is clearly shown by the particle 'al kēn (עַל־כֵּן), "therefore."

3. The term is mîšôr, which can refer to the "high plateau in the Transjordan north of Wadi Arnon" (Cogan, I Kings, 466; see also HALOT 1:578).

4. The word peḥâ appears twenty-eight times in the Hebrew of the Old Testament and another ten times in the Aramaic of the Old Testament, many of which are post-exilic contexts (HALOT 2:923, 1955–56). However, the Akkadian cognates pīḫātu and pāḫātu are ubiquitous across their respective contexts. More importantly, they display a semantic range that encompasses both administrative and military responsibilities. Based on the example of 1 Kings 20:24 (as well as 2 Kgs 18:24 and Isa 36:9), it seems clear that the Hebrew usage of the term mirrors this semantic range. The difficulty is, however, trying to determine why they replaced the məlākîm.

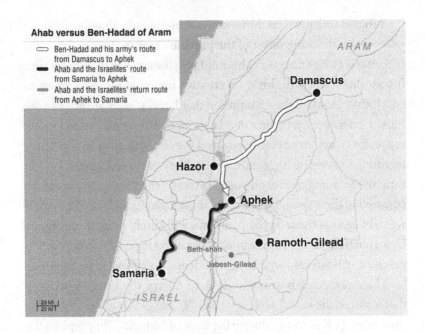

MAP 4: **Ahab versus Ben-Hadad of Aram**

for horse, chariot for chariot." So, while Aramean tactics changed, their goal remained: decisive victory over Israel.

The reader is not told if the king pondered this proposal extensively, only that he complied with the suggestions (1 Kgs 20:25b). At the turn of the year (לִתְשׁוּבַת הַשָּׁנָה, *litšûbat haššānâ*) during late spring or early summer, the newly marshalled Aramean force mobilized at Aphek. Aphek is notoriously difficult to identify. According to W. F. Albright, there are several different Apheks, and virtually all scholars still accept this general conclusion.[5] Whether the Aphek of 1 Kings 20 (20:26, 30; 2 Kgs 13:17) should be identified as Fiq, En Gev, or some other site, Aramean mobilization at this location symbolized their aggression

---

5. W. F. Albright, "One Aphek or Four?" *JPOS* 2 (1922): 184–89. Albright is responding to S. Tolkowsky, "Aphek: A Study in Biblical Topography," *JPOS* 2 (1922): 145–58. See also Robert North, "Ap(h)eq(a) and Azeqa," *Biblica* 41.1 (1960): 41–63.

and encroachment into Israelite territory. Nevertheless, En Gev is likely the best option for this context.[6] There are substantive Iron Age remains at this location, and it likely functioned as an influential social and political hub for the Arameans in the southern Levant.[7]

4.1 THE ISRAELITE ARMY: LIKE TWO SMALL FLOCKS OF GOATS?

Israel responded to the Aramean mobilization by mustering its fighting force, making provisions for battle, and encamping "opposite them" (נֶגְדָּם, negdām; 1 Kgs 20:27). In the midst of this sequence the text provides a description of the Israelite army that has perpetually perplexed scholars. In fact, it has functioned as a salient point in the argument that the battle accounts of 1 Kings 20 and 22 were original to a later context.[8] The issue is that the picture of inferiority suggested by the traditional translation of the phrase kišnê ḥăśipê ʿizzîm (כִּשְׁנֵי חֲשִׂפֵי עִזִּים) as "like two small flocks of goats" does not reflect the realities of the Omride era.[9] Given that Ahab was responsible for such a formidable force in the Syro-Palestinian coalition at Qarqar, it is perplexing that the Israelite forces would be described so diminutively. Thus, the reference to such a small army seems to betray a

---

6. Both Fiq and En Gev are located east of the Sea of Galilee in the southern portion of the Golan Heights. En Gev is also described as "Lower Aphek," presumably because it is on the eastern shore of the sea. Fiq is slightly further east, at approximately 1,100 feet above sea level. However, other proposals have included sites in the Jezreel Valley (for a survey, see Shuichi Hasegawa, "Looking for Aphek in 1 Kgs 20," VT 62 (2012): 502–4; Rasmussen, Zondervan Atlas, 275). Interestingly, Hasegawa argues that Aphek should be understood more for its rhetorical function than its historical one (Hasegawa, "Looking for Aphek in 1 Kgs 20," 501–14).

7. Moshe Kochavi, Timothy Renner, Ira Spar, and Esther Yadin, "Rediscovered: The Land of Geshur," BAR 18 (1992): 30–44. Interestingly, the Hebrew of 1 Kings 20:26 reads wayyaʿal ʾapēqâ lammilḥāmâ (וַיַּעַל אֲפֵקָה לַמִּלְחָמָה), which is often translated, "[Ben-Hadad] went up to Aphek" (e.g., NRSV, ESV, NIV, NASB). To some this may be an argument for identifying Fiq as Aphek, for it is further east and higher above sea level. However, the NLT paraphrases the sense effectively within its militaristic context: "(Ben-Hadad) marched out against Israel, this time at Aphek."

8. See, e.g., McKenzie, The Trouble with Kings, 88–89.

9. While not all translations render the phrase kišnê ḥăśipê ʿizzîm (כִּשְׁנֵי חֲשִׂפֵי עִזִּים) exactly the same, the following English versions are semantically synonymous: ESV; NABR; NASB; NIV; NKJV; NLT; NRSV.

later referent. However, there is significant reason to believe that the traditional translation misses the mark.

While translations commonly understand the phrase as referring to two "flocks," the semantic range of the root *ḥśp (חשׂף) across the Old Testament does not include the idea of "flocks."[10] Rather, its usage suggests the exposure of something by removing or stripping off a real or figurative covering (Isa 47:2; Jer 13:26; 49:10; Joel 1:7), or the action of skimming water (see Isa 30:14; Hag 2:16).

We consider it more likely that the description of two ḥśp-goats invokes specific imagery of rutting male goats. When male goats enter their mating cycles, hormones and energy consumption increases. Rutting results in increased agitation and a physiological deterioration observable in a decreased hair quality and body condition score. It is in this sense that rutting male goats, either domesticated or wild, could have an "exposed" or "stripped" demeanor—hair disheveled and of poor quality while their bones protrude through their skin. Moreover, two rutting males would certainly be inclined to spar, and the confrontation would be intense. Consequently, the image was likely that of a force smaller than their opposition but extremely agitated and eager to release pent-up energy. Our proposed translation of 1 Kings 20:27 is: "When the Israelites mustered themselves and were supplied, they went out against them. The sons of Israel encamped opposite them like two (sexually) agitated goats. As for Aram, they filled the land."

---

10. For a detailed presentation of our interpretation of this phrase, see David B. Schreiner and Kyle R. Greenwood, "An Army Like Goats: A Semantic and Zoological Reconsideration of 1 Kings 20:27," VT (published online ahead of print 2022), DOI: 10.1163/15685330-bja10094. The idea of "flock" enters the discussion through G. R. Driver's problematic proposal (G. R. Driver, "Studies in the Vocabulary of the Old Testament II," JTS 32.127 [1931]: 255). First, he argued for this reading of 1 Kings 20:27 based on his conclusions from Psalm 29:9, where the verbal form wayyeḥĕśōp (וַיֶּחֱשֹׂף) should be related to the Arabic cognate for "bleating kid." He then applied the same etymological connection to 1 Kings 20:27. Such an application does not properly consider the differences between the two passages, nor does it allow the Hebrew data to lead. Moreover, Driver's conclusions for Psalm 29:9 are by no means definitive. The Hebrew text can be explained without appealing to a late Arabic cognate. On allowing the Hebrew data to determine the contours of linguistic conversations, see James Barr, *Comparative Philology and the Text of the Old Testament* (Oxford: Clarendon Press, 1968), *passim*.

FIGURE 7: **Capra Nubiana clashing horns, a specific that may be behind the imagery of 1 Kings 20:27**

4.2 THE OUTCOME AT APHEK AND THE FATAL ERROR OF THE ISRAELITE KING

Returning to the topic at hand—the battle of Aphek—it is without question that the Israelite force was the overwhelming underdog. Nevertheless, an anonymous "man of God" (אִישׁ הָאֱלֹהִים, *ʾîš hāʾĕlōhîm*) proclaimed that such a lopsided scenario played perfectly into God's intentions, seeking to expose the fallacies of the Aramean position. Unanticipated victory, like the outcome at the siege of Samaria, was the goal because it effectively and powerfully displayed Yahweh's abilities and sphere of influence, thereby producing a universal acknowledgment of his power.

> Then a man of God approached and talked to the king of Israel. He said, "Thus says Yahweh. Because the Arameans said, 'Yahweh is a god of hills, and he is not a god of valleys,' I will give all of this great army into your hands so that you will know that I am Yahweh." (1 Kgs 20:28)

Like the siege of Samaria, there is remarkably little in the biblical account devoted to the actual battle. In 1 Kings 20:27–28, the reader is told that the precursors to war lasted over six days, but fighting broke out on the seventh day, which quickly resulted in a decisive Israelite victory. In turn, the Arameans retreated to Aphek, but unfortunately for them, the city did not offer much protection, as the wall fell upon some 27,000 men (20:29). Importantly though, Ben-Hadad was not among this unlucky mass. According to 20:30, the Aramean king found refuge inside the depths of the city, which proved to be pivotal: "But when Ben-Hadad fled, he went to the city, to a hidden room."[11]

While he was hiding in Aphek, Ben-Hadad's servants hammered out a desperate rescue plan that appealed to the reputation of the Israelite kings:

> Then his servants said to him, "Behold. We have heard about the kings of the house of Israel, that they are faithful kings. Let us put sackcloth on our waists and ropes around our heads. Let us go out to the king of Israel. Perhaps he will let your soul live." (1 Kgs 20:31)

The critical phrase in this proposal is *kî malkê bêt yiśrāʾēl kî malkê ḥesed hēm* (כִּי מַלְכֵי בֵית יִשְׂרָאֵל כִּי־מַלְכֵי חֶסֶד הֵם; "the kings of the house of Israel, that they are faithful kings"), particularly the absolute noun *ḥesed* ("faithful"). The servants of Ben-Hadad seized upon an ostensibly well-known tendency that Israelite kings prioritized rescuing diplomatic ties when the opportunity presented itself. Thus, the servants propose showing remorse through engaging a mourning ritual and throwing themselves at the mercy of the Omride king. Truth be told, it is not much of a plan. However, this account testifies that sometimes plans do not need to be overly complicated. According to 1 Kings 20:32–34, their plan worked. Not only was the Aramean king spared his execution, but he was allowed to return to Damascus and facilitate a new diplomatic arrangement.

---

11. The Hebrew phrase literally reads "a room in a room" (חֶדֶר בְּחָדֶר, *ḥeder bəḥeder*). Interestingly, this phrase will be repeated with the same governing verb *bwʾ* (בוא) in 1 Kings 22:25, when Micaiah ben Imlah pronounces judgment upon the Israelite king.

It is difficult to say who demonstrated the better political acumen. On the one hand, the servants of Ben-Hadad read the negotiations brilliantly, jumping at the opportunity to secure any outcome for their king that did not somehow involve death (1 Kgs 20:33). On the other hand, the Israelite king was able to dictate new economic footing in Aramean territory. In a quick exchange, largely initiated by the Aramean contingent, the Arameans committed to returning territory and market-share that had been lost by Israel at some point. Unfortunately, this political mediation also sealed the fate of the Israelite king. In other words, while this negotiation was politically and economically beneficial for the nation of Israel, it was personally devastating.

The consequences of this new covenant (1 Kgs 20:34) are revealed through a prophetic encounter. In one of the more perplexing interchanges in all of Scripture, an anonymous "man of God" began a process that ultimately trapped the victorious Israelite king in his blatant disobedience but required the prophet to suffer a severe beating (20:35). Yet even more perplexing is the judgment imposed upon the fellow prophet who refused to comply with the odd mandate. While it is very reasonable to reject a request for physical assault (20:36), its ethical implications are not the point. Rather, the focus is absolute obedience, which happens to align well with the overarching sense of 20:23–43. The prophet challenged the king's decision to shun obedience and responsibility for the sake of political and economic benefit. When the prophet received the necessary beating from another member of the guild, he disguised and positioned himself along the road in wait for the king's procession.

4.3 PROPHETIC CONFRONTATION
AND THE VIOLATION OF ḤĒREM

When the king passed by, the disguised prophet called out for the king to listen to his plight. In a scene that invokes Nathan's confrontation of David (2 Sam 12), this anonymous prophet narrated an account that is covertly designed to indict the king by using his own words of judgment against himself. However, whereas David's self-indictment produced repentance, there was no repentance here, only self-pity (1 Kgs 20:43). The description of the Aramean king is particularly important. Yahweh described Ben-Hadad through the prophet as "a man of my ḥērem" (אִישׁ־חֶרְמִי, 'îš ḥermî). The concept of ḥērem (חֵרֶם) is often a militaristic one that invokes a host of other concepts and ideas, such as the nebulus idea of "total victory." The king's error was that he traded negotiation for total victory. As a result, in fulfillment of the symbolic narrative given in 1 Kings 20:39–40, the king's life would be given in place of the Aramean's.

Nevertheless, it seems that the nuances of this indictment run deeper than just rejecting "total victory." For this, we must briefly consider the semantics and dynamics of the concept of ḥērem. The term ḥērem appears in multiple locations across the Old Testament, with a total of seventy-eight nominal and verbal forms.[12] One can summarize their semantics in terms of two distinct domains.[13] On the one hand, it functions within a religious domain, speaking to something used for a particular sacral purpose. It invokes ideas of holiness, and in some cases the object designated as ḥērem cannot be redeemed (see Lev 27:21).[14] On the other hand, it functions within a militaristic domain, speaking to the ostensible destruction of something or someone for a variety of reasons. And in the later prophetic traditions, this militaristic connotation has eschatological implications (see Isa 34:2; Jer 50:21, 26). Nevertheless, the militaristic connotation is without question the most prevalent across the Old Testament, although there are

---

12. Important loci for understanding this concept include Deuteronomy (1:44; 2:34; 3:6, 8, 9; 4:48; 7:2, 26; 13:15, 17–18; 20:17) and Joshua (2:10; 6:17–18, 21; 7:1, 11–15; 8:26; 10:1, 28, 35, 37, 39–40; 11:11–12, 20–21; 22:20).

13. Verslius takes these semantics a step further, arguing that the religious domain is restricted to the nominal forms of the root while the verbal forms are restricted to a militaristic connotation (Arie Verslius, "Devotion and/or Destruction? The Meaning and Function of חרם in the Old Testament," ZAW 128.2 [2016]: 234–37).

14. Verslius recognizes the relationship of ḥērem to holiness, as well as other classifications (Verslius, "Devotion and/or Destruction?," 235–36).

places where the line between the religious and militaristic domains is blurred (e.g., Josh 7–8).[15]

In a recent study, John Walton and Harvey Walton have argued for a more unified understanding of the concept of ḥērem.[16] Instead of dividing the occurrences into separate semantic domains, they argue that ḥērem merely means to remove "something from human use" and is applicable to objects, living things, abstractions, and cities: "The emphasis is not on the object but on everyone around the object. ... When ḥerem objects are destroyed, the purpose of the destruction is to make sure that nobody can use it."[17] Moreover, they are clear that while ḥērem may involve destruction, such destruction "is not the essential meaning of ḥerem because not everything that is ḥerem is destroyed."[18]

This simple framework is admittedly useful. In particular, the straightforward idea of being removed from use explains the literary conventions of certain texts that make prodigious use of this concept while suggesting that there may be more than meets the eye.[19] However, defining a very complicated concept by such a simplistic definition appears reductionist. That ḥērem shows affinities with other complex social and theological concepts presses one to ask if the basic idea of "removal from human use" does justice to the nuances involved. Perhaps then, it may be best to speak of ḥērem as a schematized word that not only defies efficient English translation but also invokes a wide array of concepts and nuances. Nevertheless,

---

15. One occurrence may defy this two-fold semantic range. In Ezra 10:8, the property of people who refused to report to Jerusalem will be ḥērem, and the offenders banned from the congregation. But even here, a religious nuance may be in view.

16. John H. Walton and J. Harvey Walton, *The Lost World of the Israelite Conquest: Covenant, Retribution, and the Fate of the Canaanites* (Downers Grove, IL: IVP Academic, 2017).

17. Walton and Walton, *Lost World of the Israelite Conquest*, 169.

18. Walton and Walton, *Lost World of the Israelite Conquest*, 170. Consequently, Walton and Walton stand against many scholars, like Verslius, who argue that destruction is inherent to the root.

19. We are thinking of Joshua's use of the concept. While seeming to communicate widespread, almost total, destruction of Canaanite settlements and populations, Joshua admits that certain towns remained to be taken and certain people groups remained in the land.

their discussion regarding Ben-Hadad's ḥērem status shows promise
for the purposes of the battle of Aphek. We will return to this shortly.

Ḥērem also appears outside the Old Testament, where the Moabite
attestation is particularly important.[20] In lines 14–18, the Moabite
Stone recounts how Mesha, at the urging of Moab's patron deity
Chemosh, moved against Nebo as a part of a larger, anti-Israel campaign. In this context, Mesha proclaims that he imposed ḥērem on
Nebo and its inhabitants for Chemosh. What is intriguing is that the
connections between ḥērem in Moabite and Israelite literature include
lexical, syntactical, and functional parallels. Syntactically, the Moabite
phrase "for I had put it to the ban for Ashtar Kemosh" (כי לאשתר
כמש החרמתה, ky l'štr kmš hḥrmth)[21] mirrors passages like Leviticus
27:28 and Joshua 6:17, where a form of the root *ḥrm is related to
a chief deity by means of a lamedh (ל) preposition.[22] Functionally,
both the Moabite and Israelite texts attest that ḥērem can be applied
to cities, and that the chief deity can be the recipient of the fruits of
those actions. All of this is akin to the book of Joshua in particular.[23]

Admittedly, the meager quantity of the data is less than ideal and is
remarkably lopsided toward an Israelite understanding. Nevertheless,
one can say that ḥērem was not uniquely an Israelite concept, even
though the literature of ancient Israel is the chief locus to study the
concept.[24] Moreover, this concept was used with tremendous ideological convictions. The thing on which ḥērem was imposed was elected
for something and chosen to function differently than it did hitherto.
It may even symbolize something else. Consequently, in the case of

---

20. Lauren A. S. Monroe, "Israelite, Moabite and Sabaean War-ḥērem Traditions and the
Forging of National Identity: Reconsidering the Sabaean Text RES 3945 in Light of Biblical
and Moabite Evidence," VT 57 (2007): 31–41.

21. KAI 181, line 17; "The Inscription of King Mesha," trans. K. D. Smelik, COS 2.23:138.

22. Leviticus employs a verbal form while Joshua employs a nominal clause: 'ak kol ḥarem
'āšer yaḥărim 'îš l-YHWH mikkol 'āšer lô (אַךְ־כָּל־חֵרֶם אֲשֶׁר יַחֲרִם אִישׁ לַיהוָה מִכָּל־אֲשֶׁר־לוֹ; Lev 27:28);
wəhayətâ hā'îr ḥērem hi' (וְהָיְתָה הָעִיר חֵרֶם הִיא וְכָל־אֲשֶׁר־בָּהּ לַיהוָה; Josh 6:17).

23. Verslius questions to what extent the Moabite Stone can be used to illuminate the Old
Testament (Verslius, "Devotion and/or Destruction?," 241).

24. On the cognate uses of ḥērem, see HALOT 1:353.

Ben-Hadad's status as divinely ḥērem-ed, Walton and Walton are on the right track when they suggest that this ḥērem status must be understood in light of his royal responsibility to embody and personify Aramean community and culture.[25] Thus, the ḥērem of Ben-Hadad as a king was also an indictment against Aramean culture and politics. In turn, this ḥērem status suggests an indirect indictment against the Israelite king, for he was exploiting the Aramean for national gain. The Israelite king was at fault because he exploited something that was to be removed from the geopolitical equation.

The Israelite king failed to take the Aramean king off the table, geopolitically speaking, but instead allowed him to remain as a prominent personality that continued to influence the landscape of Syria-Palestine. In contrast, Yahweh apparently wanted him removed from the scene (see 1 Kgs 20:28). Tragically, by negotiating and granting Ben-Hadad vassalship, the Israelite king violated the ḥērem. Moreover, like Achan (Josh 7), the Israelite king effectively assumed the same classification as ḥērem-ed.

4.4 CONCLUSIONS

Historiographically speaking, the ḥērem concept fits well with the generalizing trend evident throughout 1 Kings 20. As discussed in the previous chapter, the prophets, the Aramean king, and the Israelite king are referenced with a significant level of anonymity. This demonstrates that individual personalities are being subordinated to the institutions and, by implication, the methods of those institutions. The historiographic focus in 1 Kings 20, at least in part, is upon the mechanisms of unbridled nationalism, including territorial expansion and military engagement.[26] And when the indictments stemming from

---

25. Walton and Walton, *Lost World of the Israelite Conquest*, 203–4 n. 28.

26. Lovell has recently argued that the point is more nuanced than a critique of nationalism, expansion, and engagement. Rather, it is about Yahweh's power, and whether there are any boundaries to that power as it is linked to the larger motif of "knowing" that power (e.g., 1 Kgs 20:28; Lovell, *Kings and Exilic Identity*, 188). However, his argument assumes a contextualization of these chapters in a larger, exilic literary context. We see no reason why both conclusions

the battle of Aphek are considered, this systematic critique of royal methods becomes even starker. Aram was to be eliminated because of their policies of harassment and slanderous rhetoric. Israel was guilty of policies and methods that ignored divine commands, all for political and social gain.

cannot be legitimate, particularly if our proposal about the genesis of these episodes is correct. See our final chapter for this discussion.

Chapter 5

THE BATTLE OF RAMOTH-GILEAD

When 1 Kings 22 opens, we read that there was relative peace between Israel and Aram for three years. However, the Hebrew is more awkward than what the English translations imply: "And they dwelt for three years; there was no war between Aram and Israel" (וַיֵּשְׁבוּ שָׁלֹשׁ שָׁנִים אֵין מִלְחָמָה בֵּין אֲרָם וּבֵין יִשְׂרָאֵל, *wayyēšbû šālōš šānîm 'ên milḥāmâ bên 'ărām ûbēn yiśrā'ēl*). This is an odd way to introduce this scene, but Mordechai Cogan points out that the form *wayyēšbû* harkens back to the final verses of chapter 20 and displays affinities with the Akkadian cognate *wašābu*, "to sit down, reside and live, to be settled."[1] He offers "They stayed at home for three years" as a particularly laudable translation.[2] His suggestion also highlights a perpetual text-critical discussion regarding the sequence of 1 Kings 20–22, where the LXX witness positions the MT's chapter 21 immediately after chapter 19.

TABLE 6: Variations in the ordering of 1 Kings 19–22

MT Ordering	LXX Ordering
19 → 20 → 21 → 22	19 → 21 → 20 → 22

---

1. *CAD*, 1.2: 386.
2. Cogan, *1 Kings*, 489.

The LXX order ensures that the narratives involving Elijah and Ahab (1 Kgs 19 and 1 Kgs 21 in the MT) are kept in proximity, and if Cogan's appeal to the end of 1 Kings 20 is correct, the LXX witness may indicate an original organization, which in turn suggests that the MT exhibits redactional activity in this case. Interestingly, 21:1 in the MT begins with "And it happened after these things" (וַיְהִי אַחַר הַדְּבָרִים הָאֵלֶּה, wayyəhî 'aḥar haddəbārîm hā'ēlâ), which Cogan interprets as expressing redaction-critical affinities.[3] However, the MT's sequence is not significantly problematic, and the hendiadys "sullenly vexed" (סַר וְזָעֵף, sar wəzā'ēp) in 1 Kings 20:43 and 21:4 provide a nice connection in the chapter sequence. Ultimately, whether 1 Kings 20–22 in the MT represents the original sequence is merely tangential to this project.[4]

The more important interpretive issue is whether the three-year designation of peace is literal or formulaic (1 Kgs 22:1). Cogan argues for a "typological number."[5] However, the passages he offers in support are certainly not definitive (Gen 22:4; Exod 19:1). In contrast, Rainey proposes something more concrete, suggesting that the "three-year" timespan was the window for the battle of Qarqar.[6] Either way, the message of the passage is equally effective whether the three-year period is a precisely or imprecisely defined period of time. The point

---

3. Cogan refers to the phrase as "an editorial link" (Cogan, *I Kings*, 476).

4. To us, the issue seems largely one of preference, given the current state of scholarship. In contrast, Walter Maier argues that the MT is to be preferred because it holds to a chronological sequence that informs 1 Kings 17–22 (Walter A. Maier, III, *1 Kings 12–22*, Concordia Commentary [Saint Louis: Concordia Publishing House, 2019], 1495–96).

5. Cogan, *1 Kings*, 489. For a discussion on the potential figurative value of the number three, also see Charles Halton, "How Big Was Nineveh? Literal versus Figurative Interpretation of City Size," *BBR* 18.2 (2008): 193–207, esp. 203–4.

6. Rainey, *Sacred Bridge*, 199. One particular text from Aššur (IM 54669) appears to be important for any reconstruction and chronology of the battle of Qarqar. In this annal, Shalmaneser III recounts campaigns in each of the first sixteen years of his reign. His account of the battle is recorded in year six, concluding with the retreat of the Damascene coalition. In regnal year seven, he captured Tīl-abnī and marched to the source of the Tigris. In year eight he captured Mê-turnat and Laḥiru, and in year nine he campaigned throughout the region of Babylonia. Consequently, it is clear that Shalmaneser's military agenda was particularly aggressive and expansive. This sequence implies that the battle of Qarqar could not have been a protracted one (see Shalmaneser III A.0.102.6 [RIMA 3:32–41]).

of the passage is to introduce a change in posture after a period of non-hostility. In what follows, then, Israel is presented as the aggressor, not Aram, and this contrasts with the picture of 1 Kings 20. The battle of Ramoth-Gilead, ostensibly, was an attempt to take back territory in the Transjordanian region that had been taken by the Arameans. Beyond this, the data does not allow for more specific conclusions.[7]

With all this said, understanding the "three-years" notation as a generally defined period fits nicely with the trend toward generalization already observed throughout the Omride war accounts. Moreover, the number three is used widely across biblical Hebrew and cognate languages as an imprecise notation of time.[8] Therefore, if we must register an opinion, the three-years likely refer to an imprecisely defined, relatively short period of time.

Additionally, the destabilization by Shalmaneser III was undoubtedly a significant factor on the Israelite psyche regarding chronological contextualization. As detailed in the opening chapter of this study, Assyrian incursions into the region were relatively steady, disruptive, and progressive. It is therefore not unreasonable to conclude that Israel exploited a lull in the Assyrian advance to expose a weakness in the Aramean position. This generalized chronological marker then functions as a literary mechanism that indicates a different geopolitical context—a time when Shalmaneser and Assyria were not actively engaged in the region.[9] Nevertheless, as we shall see, the issues surrounding the battle of Ramoth-Gilead, as well as the manner in which the battle is recounted, are incredibly complex.

---

7. We are aware that 2 Kings 8:28 bears witness to later conflict between Aram and Israel surrounding the control of Ramoth-Gilead. Let it suffice to say at this point that there were multiple conflicts over this location due to the ebb and flow of the region's politics. However, as we will discuss below, certain considerations, including the textual realities of 8:28–29 and chapters 9–10, force one to consider whether the battle of Ramoth-Gilead was emphasized and applied to Ahab's context for ideological reasons.

8. In particular, see the related *šilšôm* (שִׁלְשׁוֹם; *HALOT* 2:1545–46).

9. The statement in Exodus 1:8 appears to be analogous. There the reader is told that a new pharaoh, who did not know Joseph, had come to power. Surely Hamilton is correct when he connects this passage to other times of transition (Victor P. Hamilton, *Exodus: An Exegetical Commentary* [Grand Rapids: Baker Academic, 2011], 7–8).

5.1 LOCATING RAMOTH-GILEAD

Ramoth-Gilead was an important site in the Transjordan region. According to Deuteronomy and Joshua, it was a Levitical city of refuge (Deut 4:43; Josh 20:8; 21:38). Later, during the Solomonic era, it functioned as a regional capital, overseeing the regions of Gilead and Bashaan (1 Kgs 4:13). Yet the site of Ramoth-Gilead has not been definitively identified. Dalman originally proposed el-Ḥuṣn as Ramoth-Gilead, but Nelson Glueck later argued for tell-Ramith/ Rumeith.[10] According to Glueck, the height of the tell, its Iron Age pottery, its strategic advantage, and the linguistic affinities of "Ramith" with "Ramoth" are critical considerations.[11] Subsequent scholarship accepted Glueck's argument, which ultimately led to Paul Lapp's excavations in the 1960s.[12]

Nevertheless, the consensus has not been absolute. E. A. Knauf took Glueck to task for what he believed to be shoddy linguistics, among other things.[13] As an alternative, Knauf argued for Tel er-Ramta: the stronger linguistic connection between Ramta and Ramoth-Gilead, the profile of its tell, and its proximity to more established Late Bronze settlements suggest it is a more probable location. However, Knauf's proposal cannot be verified, and thus remains overwhelmingly speculative. According to his research, Knauf claims that modern governmental institutions have not listed Ramta on the appropriate databases to ensure its protection against modern

---

10. Albright later agreed with Dalman (William F. Albright, "Bronze Age Mounds of Northern Palestine and the Hauran: The Spring Trip of the School in Jerusalem," *BASOR* 19 [1925]: 16).

11. Nelson Glueck, "Ramoth-Gilead," *BASOR* 92 (1943): 12–13.

12. Nancy L. Lapp, "Rumeith, Tell er-," in *The Oxford Encyclopedia of Archaeology in the Near East*, ed. Eric M. Meyers, 5 vols. (New York: Oxford University Press, 1997), 4:444–45; Paul W. Lapp, "Tell er-Rumeith," *RB* 70 (1963): 406–11; Lapp, "Tell er-Rumeith," *RB* 75 (1968): 98–105; Paul W. Lapp, "Excavations at Tell er-Rumeith," in *The Tale of the Tell: Archaeological Studies by Paul W. Lapp*, ed. Nancy L. Lapp and Dikran Hadidian (Eugene, OR: Pickwick, 1975), 111–19; see also Israel Finkelstein, Oded Lipschits, and Omer Sergi, "Tell er-Rumeith in Northern Jordan: Some Archaeological and Historical Observations," *Semitica* 55 (2013): 7–23.

13. Ernst Axel Knauf, "The Mists of Ramthalon: How Ramoth-Gilead Disappeared from the Archaeological Record," *BN* 110 (2001): 33–35.

development. Thus, any substantive archaeological excavation is very unlikely.[14]

Still, the problem with Glueck's proposal and the results of Lapp's excavations are the site's meager profile and remains relative to what one might expect from such a politically important site. As later admitted by Nancy Lapp: "The site's small size could disqualify the identification."[15] Nevertheless, the battle over Ramoth-Gilead is linked to its strategic value, not its size. A modest site should not necessarily preclude tell-Ramith/Rumeith.[16] As things currently stand, this site still enjoys a consensus, albeit a tentative one.

5.2 THE BATTLE OF RAMOTH-GILEAD

The strategic value of Ramoth-Gilead appears again in 1 Kings 22. The king of Israel felt compelled in his battle preparations to invoke existing covenantal prerogatives upon Jehoshaphat of Judah (1 Kgs 22:2–4). Therefore, when the Judean king utters, "I am as you are; my people are your people; my horses are your horses," he accepted the terms of his covenant with Israel.[17]

The battle in 1 Kings 22 is disrupted by a lengthy account of prophetic sparring. Beginning in 22:5, Jehoshaphat presses the king of

---

14. Knauf, "Mists of Ramthalon," 35–36. Finkelstein, Lipschits, and Sergi happen to agree with Knauf. However, their agreement does not diminish the speculative nature of Knauf's proposal. Rather, it seems to be the byproduct of a deconstruction of Glueck and Lapp's ideas (Finkelstein, Lipschits, and Sergi, "Tell er-Rumeith," 23).

15. Nancy Lapp, "Rumeith," 444. It bears noting that Nancy and Paul Lapp were an archaeological spousal team until Paul's premature death at the age of 39 (Edward F. Campbell, Jr., "Paul W. Lapp: In Memorium," BA 33.2 (1970): 60–62).

16. Finkelstein, Lipschits, and Sergi argue based on the analogy with sites like Jabesh-Gilead and Mizpah of Gilead. They also appeal to the assumption that a site with such political prominence should exhibit a significant history of occupation—even if only in the Iron Age. Rather, in their eyes Ramath/Rumeith "does not fit the description," as it only exhibits evidence of occupation "for a relatively short period" (Finkelstein, Lipschits, and Sergi, "Tell er-Rumeith," 22).

17. This relationship is made explicit in 2 Chronicles 18:1–2. The biblical text never fully divulges the dynamics of whether it was a suzerain-vassal or a parity treaty. However, based on the archaeological record of Samaria vis-à-vis the record of Jerusalem, the extrabiblical testimony (including Neo-Assyrian records), and the implications of 1 Kings 22:1–4, it is best to assume that Israel was the dominant party. For a survey of the relationship between Israel and Judah in the ninth century, see Greenwood, "Late Tenth- and Ninth-Century Issues," 286–318.

Israel to "inquire now about the word of the Lord," for Jehoshaphat seeks clarity and guidance during a time of crisis.[18] However, this initiative speaks to a characterization of Jehoshaphat that is noticeably different than what is detailed in the actual account of the battle (22:1–4; 29–38). In the battle, Jehoshaphat is passive and repeatedly described in a subordinate position, even ultimately accepting his function as a decoy with no documented rebuttal. Conversely, in 22:5–28, he appears as the more dominant character, pushing the Israelite king into an uncomfortable position with respect to the prophetic conflict between Zedekiah and Micaiah ben Imlah as the initial round of prophecies was not satisfactory (22:7). In light of these dynamics, scholars conclude that the prophetic interviews constitute a secondary addition to chapter 22.[19] In some cases, they link these materials to larger redactional programs.[20]

Seeing 1 Kings 22:5–28 as a later insertion is certainly possible, for the traditions surrounding the Israelite kings, even those associated with the Omride dynasty, likely developed over time—as we discussed for 2 Kings 9–10 in chapter 2. However, where 2 Kings 9–10 exhibits literary evidence that is widely understood to be a marker of redactional activity (i.e., repetitive resumption; *Wiederaufnahme*), similar evidence is not observable in 1 Kings 22:5–8. Moreover, merely a shift in characterization strikes us as dubious ground to see redactional activity. Nevertheless, the shifting characterization of Jehoshaphat occurs in the context of a nuanced discussion of prophetic conflict.

---

18. As Schreiner has profiled, such a time of national crisis was a context in which the prophetic office functioned most naturally (Schreiner, *Pondering the Spade*, 30–34).

19. Most notably, Ernst Würthwein, "Zur Komposition von I Reg 22:1–38," in *Das ferne und nahe Wort: Festschrift Leonhard Rost zur Vollendung seines 70 Lebenjahres am 31.11.66 gewidmet*, ed. F. Maass, BZAW 105 (Berlin: Walter de Gruyter, 1967); Würthwein, *Die Bücher der Könige: I Kön. 17–II Kön. 25*, Das Alte Testament Deutsch 11.2 (Göttingen: Vandenhoeck & Ruprecht, 1984), 253–57; see also Hans Christoph Schmitt, *Elisa: Traditionsgeschichtliche Untersuchungen zur vorklassichen nordisraelitischen Prophetie* (Gütersloh: Gütersloher Verlagshaus, 1972), 42–45.

20. Omer Sergi, "The Battle of Ramoth-gilead and the Rise of the Aramean Hegemony in the Southern Levant during the Second Half of the 9th Century BC," in *Wandering Arameans: Arameans Outside Syria; Textual and Archaeological Perspectives*, eds. Angelika Berlejung, Aren M. Maeir, and Andreas Schüle (Weisbaden: Harrassowitz Verlag, 2017), 87; see also Evangelia G. Dafni, "רוח שקר und falsche Prophetie in I Reg 22," ZAW 112 (2000): 365–85.

While the passage indeed speaks to a situation in life when the community was wrestling with the realities of conflicting advice—and the ninth century BC with its political ebbs and flows certainly fits the bill—there is also a theme of divine deception added to the equation (22:19–23), which certainly adds to the dynamics. If Evangelia Dafni is correct, the spirit of deception in the passage not only speaks to a well-defined theology of prophecy, but also displays affinities with prophetic obstacles featured later in periods of the divided monarchy.[21] Finally, there is the realization that if 22:5–28 were omitted, the battle account would proceed undisrupted. Thus, while there are no explicit literary marks to suggest a secondary status for 22:5–28, there may be enough circumstantial evidence for such a classification.

If one denies the secondary status of 1 Kings 22:5–28, then the shift in historiographic focus further develops the critique of Omride policies that has been developing across chapters 20 and 22. Not only do the northern kings display a preference for political expediency over obedience (20:41–42), but 22:5–28 reveals a tendency to engage the prophetic institution merely as a formality and not with any serious interest. What is more, the critique is intensified by the juxtaposition of Jehoshaphat with the anonymous king of Israel.[22] By explicitly naming Jehoshaphat six times while referring to the "king of Israel" seven times, 22:5–28 positions Jehoshaphat as the object of emulation while relegating his royal counterpart to a mere institution. This impressive rhetoric characterizes kings who consult Yahweh merely as a formality not even worth naming.

The account of the battle resumes in 1 Kings 22:29, and final preparations are made as the Israelite coalition approaches Ramoth-Gilead:

---

21. Dafni, "שקר רוח und falsche Prophetie," 385. Dafni argues that the conflict between Micaiah ben Imlah and Zedekiah resembles the conflicts of Micah, Jeremiah, and Ezekiel. However, she emphasizes Micaiah ben Imlah's uniqueness exists in the tracing of false prophecy back to a deceptive spirit.

22. Most notably, Jehoshaphat is one of seven kings of the united monarchy (all from Judea) identified by the Deuteronomist as having "done what was right in the eyes of the Lord" (Asa, 1 Kgs 15:9–15; Jehoshaphat, 22:41–45; Amaziah, 2 Kgs 14:1–6; Jotham, 15:32–38; Azariah, 16:1–7; Hezekiah, 18:1–8; Josiah, 22:1–2).

the Israelite king resolves "to disguise himself" (הִתְחַפֵּשׂ, *hithap-pēś*) while Jehoshaphat is commanded to wear his own clothes (וְאַתָּה לְבַשׁ בְּגָדֶיךָ, *wə'attâ ləbaš bəgādêkā*). Clearly the Israelite king is again dictating terms, and Jehoshaphat complies.[23] Such a pecking order recalls the dynamics of 22:1–4, as well as the likely historical reality that Jehoshaphat had entered into a treaty with Ahab (see above). Most importantly, the Israelite king's plan works, at least initially, for he caught the eye of enemy force and secured its pursuit. However, Jehoshaphat's instinct for self-preservation won out: "When the commanders of the chariotry saw Jehoshaphat, they said, 'Surely he is the king of Israel!' So, they turned against him to fight. Then Jehoshaphat cried out. When the commanders of the chariotry saw that he was not the king of Israel, they retreated from him" (22:32).

According to 1 Kings 22:31, the Aramean king gave his forces strict orders to identify and neutralize the king of Israel. Apparently, the Aramean-led force believed that if the leader of the opposition were deposed then victory would inevitably follow. Such logic is reasonable, but in this case, it proved to be too arduous. In their zealous pursuit of the Israelite king, the force mistakenly identified Jehoshaphat as the Israelite king based on superficial appearance. Yet to their credit, they broke off their pursuit upon realizing their misidentification. Ironically, however, they were successful, though they did not immediately realize it. The text goes on to recount, in vivid detail, that an anonymous archer unknowingly mortally wounded the Israelite king: "Now when a man innocently pulled back his bow, he struck the king of Israel between the layers of armor.[24] So he said to his chariot driver, 'Turn around and take me from the theater of battle for I am wounded'" (22:34).

---

23. "An individual of higher social status is more likely to address one of lower social status with the regular imperative than with another type of imperative" (Hélène Dallaire, *The Syntax of Volitives in Biblical Hebrew and Amarna Canaanite Prose*, Linguistic Studies in Ancient West Semitic 9 [Winona Lake, IN: Eisenbrauns, 2014], 88).

24. The nouns *haddəbāqîm* (הַדְּבָקִים) and *haširîn* (הַשִּׁרְיָן) appear as a hendiadys, particularly since they exhibit overlapping semantic domains (*HALOT* 1:209; 2:1655).

The image created in the text is that of random chance. However, the reader is privy to the wider conversation, whereby an Aramean arrow was divinely guided to the weakness in the king of Israel's armor, fulfilling the prophetic word of the anonymous prophet and of Micaiah ben Imlah (1 Kgs 20:41–42; 22:28). As described by Keith Bodner: "The narrative does not explicitly announce that God has directed the arrow, but the reader is invited to conclude that a hidden guidance system is at work."[25] In the case of Micaiah ben Imlah, he is also proven to be the legitimate prophet of Yahweh (22:11).

The Israelite king eventually died on the battlefield, bleeding out as he watched the fighting unfold. And when this happened, a cry of retreat echoed throughout the Israelite ranks: "A cry went through the camp when the sun set saying, 'Each man to his city; each man to his land!'" (1 Kgs 22:36). Thus, the Arameans maintained control of Ramoth-Gilead by successfully repulsing the Israelite-Judean coalition. Moreover, the last image is that of an Israelite king's blood being licked by dogs and the people washing his blood-soaked chariot by the pool of Samaria as prostitutes bathe. It is a shameful image of wild scavengers made worse by the grisly image of prostitutes bathing in bloodied waters.[26] When 1 Kings 22 ends with the typical notations of Ahab's reign, achievements, and successors, the reader cannot help but feel relieved. Mundane administrative details are welcome in place of these unsettling images.

At this point, there are several historical questions that must be entertained. Who was the king of Israel in 1 Kings 22? Was it Ahab,

---

25. Keith Bodner, *The Theology of the Book of Kings*, Old Testament Theology (Cambridge: Cambridge University Press, 2019), 128.

26. Cogan notes the juxtaposition of dogs and pigs in certain Neo-Assyrian curse formulas, and he ponders if "prostitutes," *hazzonōt*, is an unintentional alteration of "pigs," *ḥăzîrîm*, particularly in light of the LXX tradition. This change is possible since the consonants can be logically confused. Moreover, the parallel to Esarhaddon's treaties (538b) supports this shift. However, the MT is coherent, although very disturbing. It is likely that the LXX translator altered the text due to its grisly detail (Cogan, *1 Kings*, 494). As for the MT, the Hebrew literally reads: "They washed the chariot by the Pool of Samaria. The dogs licked his blood and the prostitutes bathed according to the word which the Lord spoke." The picture painted, therefore, is one of prostitutes bathing in waters bloodied by the deceased.

or was it a later king only to have Ahab added at a later time? How
many battles of Ramoth-Gilead were there? What does one make of
the Omrides after Ahab's death? What was the sequence of succeed-
ing kings, and what was their relationship to the Judean kings after
Jehoshaphat? These questions are all linked, but we will begin with
a discussion about the battle of Ramoth-Gilead.

5.3 THE BATTLE (OR BATTLES) OF RAMOTH-GILEAD AND ISRAELITE ROYALTY

We have already mentioned that the location of Ramoth-Gilead has
proven difficult to identify. The dynamics of the conflicts that took
place there between the Israelites and the Arameans are also difficult
to interpret. The book of Kings boasts three distinct contexts where
Israelite and Aramean conflict appears near Ramoth-Gilead (1 Kgs
22; 2 Kgs 8:29; 9:1–13), suggesting multiple engagements. However, if
one accepts any redactional program suggesting Ahab was fixed to a
tradition from another period of Israelite history, then all bets are off.
There may have been only one conflict, but there may have also been
more. Moreover, if one concedes that the Tel Dan Stele is witness to
an Israelite and Aramean conflict around Ramoth-Gilead, then yet
another voice that speaks about Israelite/Aramean conflict in the vicinity of Ramoth-Gilead must be considered, complicating things further.

Omer Sergi argues that the Tel Dan Stele refers to, without explicitly mentioning them, the events of Ramoth-Gilead memorialized in
2 Kings. The stele is a co-witness to the events documented in 2 Kings
8:28–29 and 2 Kings 9: "The only known battle in which Joram and
Ahaziah confronted Hazael of Damascus is the battle of Ramoth-
gilead and thus it is certainly possible that the Aramean inscription
from Dan refers to the events of 842/41 BC."[27] He focuses on lines
three through four of the inscription for support, where the term *qdm*
(קדם) is often taken as "previously," suggesting Israelite aggression

---

FIGURE 8: **The Tel Dan Stele, angle view**

prior to the Aramean's installation as king. However, Sergi acknowledges some difficulties with the traditional rendering. First, *qdm* is not normally an adverb, and rendering it as such produces an awkward dynamic with the previous verbs. Nevertheless, rendering *qdm* as a toponym is also problematic. Ultimately, Sergi focuses on the sequence implied by numerous proposals that understand *qdm* adverbially, for he sees continuity with Kings. He concludes: "The king of Israel invaded after the death of Hazael's predecessor, but before his own coronation."[28] Sergi believes that J(eh)oram took advantage of Damascus's power transfer to invade Aramean territory.

---

28. Sergi, "Battle of Ramoth-gilead," 85.

Admittedly, this creates a tight chronological window for Israel to invade Aramean controlled territory, but Sergi argues such a window aligns nicely with the inscription's apologetic purpose. A tight time-line, according to Sergi, suggests a volatile geopolitical situation, and Hazael, who is apparently celebrated on the stele, was able to cope with these intense regional politics and geopolitical maneuvering. This timeline is critical to Sergi's reconstruction of events, as well as the relationship between the inscriptional and biblical testimonies.[29]

Sergi's proposal is intriguing. It properly considers the apologetic nature of the inscription as well as the grammatical nuances of the inscriptional text. However, there is not much to work with. Even if he is correct in proposing that the inscription is referring to Israelite encroachment, a reference to Ramoth-Gilead is circumstantial at best. In spite of this, we are inclined to tentatively accept that the battle of Ramoth-Gilead is alluded to in the Tel Dan Stele. In short, what other possibilities are there with which to work? Nevertheless, the stele appears to bear definitive witness to Israelite encroachment upon Aramean territory during the middle of the ninth century.

The biblical testimony regarding the conflicts at Ramoth-Gilead is just as difficult, but for different reasons. Consider 2 Kings 8:28–29:

> When he [Ahaziah] went with J(eh)oram,[30] son of Ahab, to battle against Hazael, king of Aram, at Ramoth-Gilead, the Arameans struck J(eh)oram. So, King J(eh)oram returned to Jezreel to heal from the blows which the Arameans struck at Ramah when he battled Hazael, king of Aram. So, Ahaziah, son of J(eh)oram, king of Judah, went down to see J(eh)oram, son of Ahab, in Jezreel because he was injured.

---

29. According to Sergi, "Indeed, historical reconstruction based on a royal apologetic inscription should be treated with caution. Yet, it is the peculiar narration of the order of events in lines 3–4, which conceals the possibility that Hazael himself was the king attacked by the King of Israel, that implies that this is exactly the way things were" (Sergi, "Battle of Ramoth-gilead," 85).

30. As mentioned earlier, this name is spelled two different ways in biblical Hebrew (see page 3 n. 1). In 2 Kings 8:28–29 the MT spells the Israelite king's name as *yôrām* and the Judahite king's name as *yəhôrām*.

Many interpreters note an ostensible tension between 2 Kings 8:28 and 8:29. According to 8:28, Ahaziah went with J(eh)oram into battle at Ramoth-Gilead against Hazael, but according to 8:29, Ahaziah went to visit the wounded J(eh)oram in Jezreel. Thus, as exemplified in the words of Sergi: "The assertion in 2 Kgs 8:28 that Ahaziah sided with Joram contradicts the continuation of the same account in the next verse (2 Kgs 8:29), where it is stated that Ahaziah has just joined Joram at Jezreel."[31] However, "contradiction" is an unfortunate description, particularly since the textual dynamics are rather complicated.

As we discussed in our second chapter, 2 Kings 8:29 is echoed in 9:15a, where we concluded that these passages likely constitute a clausal resumption, suggesting that the prophetic anointing of Jehu while he is stationed at Ramoth-Gilead is a secondary insertion within the larger narrative. By implication, what Sergi considers a contradiction is likely associated with the diachronic realities of the text. And given that the disjunctive clause noting Ahaziah's visitation follows the proposed clausal resumption, it is possible to understand the final clause of 8:29—the clause that Sergi seizes to point out the contradiction—as an explanatory statement explaining why Ahaziah eventually accompanied J(eh)oram in confrontation of Jehu (9:21). Thus, any tension inherent to the juxtaposition of 8:28 and 8:29 is the byproduct of the effort to alleviate any confusion materializing later in the narrative's development. More importantly, these diachronic considerations also suggest that the battle of Ramoth-Gilead became an optimal context for socio-political and theological commentary.[32] What was originally discussed in terms of geo-politics was later given a prophetic component, rooting Jehu's bloody coup in divine sanction, and it is precisely this attraction that may explain the poetics and function of 1 Kings 22.

---

31. Sergi, "Battle of Ramoth-gilead," 86.

32. Bodner reflects this emphasis: "As it stands, the quarrel over Ramoth-Gilead gives rise to a number of theological questions and conundrums, such as the issue of true versus false prophecy, the possibility of divine deception, and the fulfillment of Elijah's word concerning Ahab's doom" (Bodner, *Theology of the Book of Kings*, 125).

In our second chapter, we also suggested that the general anonymity in 1 Kings 20 and 22 is a literary and historiographic convention. We argued that the anonymization functions within a broader historiographic trend and in the context of 1 Kings relegates any specific criticism of Ahab under a larger critique aimed at the dynasty's political *modus operandi*. However, in that discussion we also suggested that general anonymization may signal external source material. With this in mind, we propose a similar historiographic function in 1 Kings 22 that not only signals a criticism of the Omride dynasty personified in Ahab but indicates that the battle of Ramoth-Gilead has been utilized to frame the historian's dynastic criticism.[33]

Of course, this suggestion raises a question. How many battles of Ramoth-Gilead were there? If there was one, then questions about historical veracity in the text naturally follow, questions that have proven to be incendiary within certain scholastic and theological traditions. To begin with, it must be acknowledged that ancient Near Eastern history writing is a rather sophisticated endeavor. Studies have shown that multiple claims about a singular event are likely linked to both political and ideological concerns.[34] Moreover, ancient Near Eastern scribes used historical events in ways that served a

---

33. Indeed, this connection is a subtle trigger, but it is not without parallel. Jonathan Grossman argues that the cumulative force of a series of "dynamic analogies" across Esther compel the reader to move beyond a surface level reading to a deeper one that comments on several social institutions, social dynamics, and theological concepts (Jonathan Grossman, *Esther: The Outer Narrative and the Hidden Reading*, Siphrut 6 [Winona Lake, IN: Eisenbrauns, 2011], 218–46). In this proposal, a historical awareness takes the place of a literary awareness. Consequently, the idea of "bringing forward" the setting of Ramoth-Gilead should not be understood as a fabrication or an invention. As we will state further below, it is about clarifying a setting to establish a connection for historiographic purposes.

34. In a well-known example, both Shalmaneser V and Sargon II claim to have sacked Samaria. The debate is ongoing, and there are as many as six possibilities according to Elayi (*Sargon II*, 48–50). Ultimately, it seems clear that Sargon came to the throne in a context that can only be described as uncertain. Elayi describes the ascent of Sargon as not that of a usurper but as the brother of his royal predecessor, Shalmaneser. However, Shalmaneser's death is shrouded in uncertainty, and there are hints of an awkward succession. Sargon, it seems, sought to make a sharp distinction between him and his predecessor. Claiming the sacking of Samaria established the right trajectory for Sargon to present himself as a warrior-king (Elayi, *Sargon II*, 25–32).

particular ideology.[35] In the case of the battle of Ramoth-Gilead, the geographic continuity between 1 Kings 22 and 2 Kings 8–10 suggests that the historian may have highlighted the context of Ramoth-Gilead as a way to comment on the life span and complexity of Israelite and Aramean relations. On the one hand, Israelite and Aramean relations were taken to new heights with Omride policy. On the other hand, when the relationship fractured because of a shift in Israelite and Aramean policies, signaled by the respective coups of Jehu and Hazael, the aftershocks threatened to consume the region and eventually the vitality of the Davidic dynasty (2 Kgs 11). When the historian highlighted the context of Ramoth-Gilead, a connection was created in the audience's mind, so that when they envisioned the accounts of Jehu's coup and the violent aftermath, they were reminded that this crisis had its genesis in Omride policy. This connectedness was not a historical misstep or an endeavor to pull the wool over the eyes of the audience. It was a historiographic decision born out of critical historical assessment.[36]

Nevertheless, it is certainly possible—given the fluid socio-political environment and Neo-Assyrian aspirations—that Ahab did indeed tussle with the Arameans over Ramoth-Gilead. The time between each wave of Neo-Assyrian advance across the southern Levant was a prime moment to reassert dominance in the region—at the expense

---

35. In a classic study, Mordechai Cogan and Hayim Tadmor have showed how Ashurbanipal's negotiations with Gyges, king of Lydia, were presented, edited, and represented in a way that eventually communicated a rather clear message: rebellion will result in death (Mordechai Cogan and Hayim Tadmor, "Gyges and Ashurbanipal: A Study in Literary Transmission," *Orientalia* 46.1 [1977]: 65–85).

36. We are reminded of F. Charles Fensham's assessment of the presentation of Ezra 4: "[H]e is referring in this chapter in chronological order to the hindrances placed in the way of the Jews to rebuild the temple and the wall of Jerusalem. When he discussed the problems of building the temple in 4:1–5, *it reminded him of later similar troubles with the rebuilding of the wall of Jerusalem*, and so 4:6–23 has been inserted, almost parenthetically, before the argument of the building of the temple has again been taken up in 4:24ff." (F. Charles Fensham, *The Books of Ezra and Nehemiah*, NICOT [Grand Rapids: Eerdmans, 1983], 70; emphasis added). With respect to 1 Kings 22, the historian, who is writing outside the sequence of events, compels the reader to see certain connections. Thus, the contextualization at Ramoth-Gilead is a quasi-parenthetical comment that sets the table for the reader to make these connections.

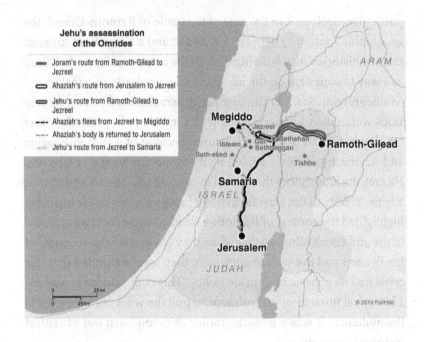

Jehu's assassination of the Omrides

- Joram's route from Ramoth-Gilead to Jezreel
- Ahaziah's route from Jerusalem to Jezreel
- Jehu's route from Ramoth-Gilead to Jezreel
- Ahaziah's flees from Jezreel to Megiddo
- Ahaziah's body is returned to Jerusalem
- Jehu's route from Jezreel to Samaria

MAP 5: **Jehu's assassination of the Omrides**

of the Arameans. Israelite and Aramean cooperation during the battle of Qarqar should not be taken as evidence that Ahab would otherwise not spar with the Arameans over territory.

5.4 THE SEQUENCE OF RULERS ASSOCIATED WITH THE OMRIDE DYNASTY

There is one final historical difficulty associated with the battle of Ramoth-Gilead that bears upon this project. The sequence of rulers in Israel after the death of Ahab's son Ahaziah, as well as the sequence of his Judean contemporaries, is notoriously difficult to understand. The traditional arrangement is as follows.

Israel: Omri → Ahab → Ahaziah → J(eh)oram

Judah: Jehoshaphat → J(eh)oram → Ahaziah

According to 2 Kings 1:17, J(eh)oram became king of Israel during
the second year of Judah's king J(eh)oram, after the death of Ahaziah,
Ahab's son: "And so, he (Ahaziah) died according to the word of the
Lord which Elijah spoke. J(eh)oram became king in his place in the
second year of J(eh)oram, son of Jehoshaphat, king of Judah, because
he did not have a son." However, 8:16 states that J(eh)oram of Judah
ascended to the throne in the fifth year of J(eh)oram of Israel: "In
the fifth year of J(eh)oram, son of Ahab king of Israel, J(eh)oram
son of Jehoshaphat became king of Judah." Consequently, these two
passages present the reader with a significant conundrum. How can
J(eh)oram of Israel ascend the throne during the reign of J(eh)oram
of Judah, only to see J(eh)oram of Judah ascend the throne during
his own reign?

This specific problem must be considered within the larger discussion regarding the genealogical difficulties associated with Israelite
and Judean kings during the ninth and eighth centuries.[37] These
well-documented issues regarding age alignments, birth orders, syn-
chronisms, and semantic ambiguity are explained text-critically and
by the assumption of co-regencies. In addition, aspects of the discussion consider potential dialectical differences between Israelite and
Judean Hebrew.[38] Essentially, one must determine whether there were
indeed multiple J(eh)orams and Ahaziahs, or if the biblical historian,
erroneously or intentionally, presented two kings with the same name
ruling at approximately the same time.

Arguments that J(eh)oram and/or Ahaziah have been incorrectly
duplicated in the biblical witness are dictated by a related debate. Was
J(eh)oram an Israelite who came to rule over Judah or vice-versa?
Philip Davies and John Rogerson argue that it makes better sense that
J(eh)oram was an Israelite member of the "dominant" Omride dynasty
who eventually "usurped the throne of Jerusalem" during the reign

---

37. Donald V. Etz, "The Genealogical Relationships of Jehoram and Ahaziah and Ahaz
and Hezekiah, Kings of Judah," *JSOT* 71 (1996): 39–53.

38. See page 3 n. 1.

of Jehoshaphat.[39] Moreover, they argue that the twenty-five years of Jehoshaphat "tallies exactly with the eighteen remaining years of Ahab, two of Ahaziah, and five of Joram."[40] However, Miller and Hayes, as well as John Strange, argue for a single Judean J(eh)oram who came to rule over Israel with the help of his wife Athaliah, an Omride princess.[41] For these three authors, it is significant that the J(eh)oram who reigned after Ahaziah, son of Ahab, is not described in the MT as "his brother." They hypothesize that J(eh)oram of Judah, under the approval of Athaliah, moved to effectively unify the divided monarchies, and when his son also named Ahaziah came of age, J(eh)oram placed him on the throne in Jerusalem, essentially as a subordinate to him in Samaria. When Jehu killed J(eh)oram and Ahaziah, Athaliah and what remained of the Omride dynasty was left to assume power in Jerusalem. Samaria at that point was under Jehu's control, and the existing Davidic dynasty stood in the way of Omride continuation, resulting in her violent purge of the Davidic family.

If the scenario of a single J(eh)oram and/or Ahaziah is accepted, then it may explain certain peculiarities in the historical record. It is curious that the text lacks the normal source citations within the regnal framework for J(eh)oram and Ahaziah. Moreover, the MT of 2 Kings 1:17 appears to preserve a reading that later textual traditions tried to clarify. The LXX and the Syriac traditions include the phrase "his brother," making it clear that J(eh)oram of Israel was the brother of Ahaziah. Thus, in the minds of those who argue for a single J(eh)oram and/or Ahaziah, the historical record is muddied by historians who failed to clarify that there was only one king discussed in two royal contexts who reigned over both Israel and Judah.

However, the problem with all these proposals is that they are incredibly speculative. Both Donald Etz and Boyd Barrick present

39. Philip R. Davies and John Rogerson, *The Old Testament World*, 2nd ed. (Louisville: Westminster John Knox, 2005), 77–78.

40. Davies and Rogerson, *Old Testament World*, 78.

41. Miller and Hays, *History of Ancient Israel and Judah*, 320–22; Strange, "Joram, King of Israel and Judah," 191–201.

possible genealogical scenarios but with a dizzying number of contingencies.[42] In turn, one wonders if these proposals actually produce more questions than answers. Miller, Hayes, Strange, and those like them, have the benefit of relative simplicity vis-à-vis other elaborate proposals, but leave one to ponder whether the details glossed over are enough to destabilize their thesis.

Lovell has offered another way to explain the difficulties, arguing that the tension arises because of an editorial process that brought together what he calls "Inner and Outer Kings." According to Lovell, these narrative blocks were written by different people from different perspectives but were eventually fused together to comment historically on the realities of Israelite history in Iron II. Thus, the appearance of two Ahaziahs and J(eh)orams is the result of an editorial awkwardness.[43] Nevertheless, all these proposals—no matter how complex—arise because of the unquestionable difficulty observed in the text. In other words, the text encourages elaborate explanations. Consequently, a primary question that must be answered concerns how far the historian or interpreter is willing to go. How much ambiguity and postulation is one willing to accept?

In our case, we do not feel the conundrum can be explained in a satisfactorily manner given the data that is currently available. What we will say is that the Tel Dan Stele appears to testify to J(eh)oram as king of Israel and Ahaziah as king of Judah, although documentation of each king's father must be reconstructed. That it references both kings in this context suggests a close geopolitical relationship between the Omride and Davidic dynasties, which is a reality that the book of Kings readily admits, but anything beyond this generalization quickly becomes dubious. Consequently, this historical difficulty will persist until new evidence provides clarification.

---

42. W. Boyd Barrick, "Another Shaking of Jehoshaphat's Family Tree: Jehoram and Ahaziah Once Again," *VT* 51.1 (2001): 9–25; Etz, "Genealogical Relationships," 39–53.

43. Lovell, *Kings and Exilic Identity*, 63. See Lovell's argument on the fusion of "Inner and Outer Kings" throughout his monograph.

5.5 CONCLUSIONS

First Kings 22 presents the interpreter with a particularly difficult set of issues. In addition to the general anonymity of the Israelite king, there are also the difficulties surrounding Ramoth-Gilead and the potential literary development of the chapter. What is without question, however, is that 1 Kings 22 represents the continuation of 1 Kings 20, which ended with judgment against Ahab for his unwillingness to fulfill *ḥērem* expectations. The opening calm of 1 Kings 22 is followed by Ahab's dynasty plunged into turmoil and transition. As anticipated by two prophets, judgment fell upon Ahab during his ambitious offensive to take control of Ramoth-Gilead, where he suffered a mortal wound and died.

We have also proposed that the battle of Ramoth-Gilead was highlighted in the narrative because it presented a wonderful opportunity to comment on Omride policy. Conflicts over Ramoth-Gilead proved to be more than just efforts to extend socio-political dominance into the Transjordanian region in a geopolitical context defined by dramatic swings of allegiance and ambitions. Rather, these conflicts became symbolic of a disastrous policy that eventually consumed the region and posed the single greatest threat to the endurance of the Davidic dynasty. By connecting the Golden Age of the Omride dynasty to its final days through Ramoth-Gilead, the historian demonstrates that the roots of dynastic tragedy were established in Omride policies that valued political expedience over covenantal fidelity and obedience to the word of Yahweh. Thus, Ahab, as the celebrated figurehead of the Omride dynasty, also becomes the author of its demise.[44]

---

44. Ahab's death is difficult for at least two reasons. First, there is the relationship between the account of his death in 1 Kings 22 with 1 Kings 21:20–29, where Elijah presents an oracle of judgment declaring the impossibility of an enduring dynasty for the Omrides. This judgment is linked to Ahab's unjust and immoral actions against Naboth. Second, the violent death of 22:35–38 is often understood to be in tension with 22:39–40, which states that Ahab "slept with his fathers." In the case of the first issue, it must be emphasized that Elijah's oracle of judgment targets a perpetual dynasty (see Jeroboam I's oracle of judgment in 14:7–16). Elijah revealed to Ahab that his family's rule was on borrowed time, where such an announcement must have been shocking given their achieved status. As for the second issue, the tension between 22:35–38 and 22:39–40 persists only with a faulty understanding of the death notice.

To be clear, we do not suggest that the historian fabricated a conflict at Ramoth-Gilead during Ahab's day. Rather, contextualizing the pivotal battle that occurred during the reign of J(eh)oram of Israel with Ahab's exploits was possible because there were likely many such conflicts between the Arameans and the Israelites over mutually desired territory. It is easy to see how Ahab would have experienced skirmishes with the Arameans during the lulls in the Neo-Assyrian advance. It was through this general reality that the historian explicitly connected the two eras within Omride history to make his point.

Therefore, we do not believe the general anonymization in 1 Kings 22, and 1 Kings 20 for that matter, is indicative of a large-scale redactional scheme that sought to apply later events to Ahab. Instead, it is better to see it as a subtle literary convention that seeks to relegate the person, in this case, Ahab, under a larger critique of his dynastic policies. Specific mention of Ahab occurs sparsely but enough to remind the reader who is inspiring the criticism.

For example, Na'aman argues that the phrase "slept with his fathers" refers to a "peaceful death" (Nadav Na'aman, "Prophetic Stories as Sources for the Histories of Jehoshaphat and the Omrides," *Biblica* 78 [1997]: 168). However, Na'aman is forced to admit that Ahab is the lone exception to the rule. As Cogan implies in his argument, this interpretation is awkward (Cogan, *1 Kings*, 495–96, esp. 496 n. 2). However, if the phrase "slept with his fathers" refers to an expected transition between kings, the difficulty dissolves. Every instance of this phrase in the book of Kings recounts an expected transition to the next monarch (1 Kgs 2:10; 11:43; 14:20, 31; 15:8, 24; 16:6, 28; 22:40, 51; 2 Kgs 8:24; 10:35; 13:9, 13; 14:6, 29; 15:7, 22, 38; 16:20; 20:21; 21:18; 24:6). One may argue that 1 Kings 2:10 runs counter to this idea. There the text reveals that David slept with his fathers, which ultimately led to a violent transition of power. However, the key is understanding an *expected* transition of power, which is not necessarily synonymous with peace. Andrew Knapp has recently argued that both Solomon and Adonijah possessed a legitimate claim to succeed David as king (Andrew Knapp, "The Conflict between Adonijah and Solomon in Light of Succession Practices Near and Far," *Journal of Hebrew Scriptures* 20, article 2 [2020]: 1–26, DOI: 10.5508/jhs29557).

Chapter 6

THE REVOLT OF MOAB

Second Kings opens with a shift in focus from the Omride conflicts to prophetic interactions, where the prophet Elijah returns to dominate the historical presentation. Before his miraculous ascension and passing his mantle to Elisha, Elijah confronted Ahab's successor, deriding Ahaziah for inquiring of Baal-zebub of Ekron whether he would recover from a fall.

> Ahaziah had fallen through the lattice of his upper room in Samaria, and he was injured. When he dispatched messengers, he said to them, "Go and inquire of Baal-zebub, the god of Ekron, if I will live from this injury." But the angel of the Lord spoke to Elijah the Tishbite, "Arise and go to meet the messengers of the king of Samaria. Say to them, 'Is it because there is no God in Israel that you are going to inquire of Baal-zebub, the god of Ekron? Therefore, thus says the Lord! The bed upon where you go, you will not come down from it, for you will surely die.'" (2 Kgs 1:2–4)

The prophetic word was not received well. Once Ahaziah determined the origin of the message (2 Kgs 1:6–8), he dispatched a contingent of 50 soldiers with orders to bring Elijah back to the king. The implication is obvious: they were to silence the prophet. Unfortunately, the first two groups of soldiers became victims of divine protection (1:10, 12) when the prophet called down fire from heaven upon each in turn. Apparently, calling fire from heaven was Elijah's *modus operandi* when faced with an ominous situation (see 1 Kgs 18).

The leader of the third group learned from the fate of the first two groups. Instead of persisting that Elijah should surrender, he interceded on behalf of his men, throwing himself at the prophet's feet (2 Kgs 1:13–14). Such an act was enough, for Elijah departed with the third group to reiterate his message to the king (1:15–16). As predicted, the result of all these events was the death of Ahaziah (1:17).

Second Kings 2 recounts the prophetic transition between Elijah and Elisha, which took place in the vicinity of Jericho. In turn, the Omride dynasty entered a new dispensation. Elijah gave way to Elisha as the chief prophetic voice attempting to influence the royal family. However, the new phase did not translate into a new appreciation for the prophetic office or the word of Yahweh. Rather, the events of 2 Kings 3, with their striking similarity to 1 Kings 22, suggest that while some things changed, most things remained the same.[1]

Second Kings 3 opens with the ascension formula, one of three elements providing the regnal framework device in the book of Kings.[2] In 3:1–3, the text discloses that J(eh)oram assumed the Israelite throne, and, interestingly, he is said to have engaged in some type of religious reform, although it was apparently not significant:

> J(eh)oram did evil in the eyes of the Lord, only not as his father and as his mother. He removed the altar of the Baal which his

---

1. The connections between 1 Kings 22 and 2 Kings 3 have long been recognized by scholars. Their interconnections include the characterization and role of Jehoshaphat, particularly as he seeks an authentic prophet prior to military engagement, phraseology, Israelite aggression, and the debate among the leadership regarding the content of the prophetic word. Recently, Lovell has argued for a sophisticated "narrative analogy" (Lovell, *Kings and Exilic Identity*, 46–47).

2. On the basic elements of the regnal framework, see Leuchter and Lamb, *Historical Writings*, 271; Wiseman, *1 and 2 Kings*, 49–55; see also David B. Schreiner, "'Now Rehoboam, Son of Solomon, Reigned in Judah': Considering the Structural Divisions of Kings and the Significance of 1 Kgs 14:21," *Journal of Inductive Biblical Studies* 7.1 (2020): 7–33.

father made. However, he clung to the sins of Jeroboam, son
of Nebat, which he caused Israel to sin. He did not remove
any of them. (2 Kgs 3:2-3)

It seems J(eh)oram is recognized as a more moderate Omride
king, at least with respect to select policies. Baalism was weakened,
but strict Yahwism still floundered under the influence of a more
questionable form of Yahwism centered on two shrines with golden
calves (1 Kgs 12:25-33).

6.1 THE REBELLION OF MESHA

With the exception of the next conflict at Ramoth-Gilead (2 Kgs
8:28-29), the final Omride conflict is recounted, beginning in 3:4.
King Mesha of Moab "rebelled" (פָּשַׁע, pšʿ) against his Omride sov-
ereigns in the wake of Ahab's death.[3] Mesha is described as a "shep-
herd" (נֹקֵד, nōqēd), which explains why his vassalship required the
supply of a large number of domesticated sheep.[4] According to the text,
his annual tribute was a massive 100,000 lambs and wool from 100,000
rams. Regardless of whether these terms are inflated or not, his rebellion would have represented a significant blow to the Omride bottom
line.[5] However, the audience is not precisely told when the rebellion

---

3. This revolt exemplifies a general historical axiom. The death of a strong leader often
provided opportunity for a shift in power, encouraging royal coups or vassal rebellions (e.g.,
2 Sam 1-3; 1 Kgs 1-3; 15:25-16:23). Successors occasionally preempted rebellion by flexing their
muscles (e.g., Exod 1:8-10; 1 Kgs 11:41-12:19). In a classic example of preemptive action, the
Neo-Assyrian king Esarhaddon enacted treaties on his vassals on behalf of the crown prince
Ashurbanipal (Donald J. Wiseman, "The Vassal-Treaties of Esarhaddon," *Iraq* 20.1 [1958]: 1-99
+ plates).

4. On the meaning of *nōqēd*, see Peter C. Craigie, *Ugarit and the Old Testament* (Grand
Rapids: Eerdmans, 1982), 71-73.

5. Sheep were extremely valuable, functioning as both a source of raw material (wool) and a
source of food and sacrifice (Roland K. Harrison and Edwin M. Yamauchi, "Animal Husbandry,"
in the *Dictionary of Daily Life in Biblical and Post-biblical Antiquity*, ed. Edwin M. Yamauchi and
Marvin R. Wilson [Peabody: Hendrickson, 2014], 1:54-55). Borowski linked diet to the sacri-
ficial system, arguing that herding was the second most important aspect of Israelite daily life.
However, presuming that herding was not a focal point of resource allocation in urban centers,
it is reasonable to speculate that Mesha's operation was the single source for their importation,
making his rebellion all the more egregious (Obed Borowski, *Daily Life in Biblical Times*, ABS 5

occurred, only that it happened "when Ahab died" (וַיְהִי כְּמוֹת אַחְאָב,
wayyəhî kəmôt 'aḥ'āb). This rebellion resulted in J(eh)oram's mar-
shalling of Judah and Edom.

Second Kings 3:6 presents J(eh)oram as a king on a mission. He
"goes out" (וַיֵּצֵא, *wayyēṣē'*) from Samaria, "marshals" troops (וַיִּפְקֹד,
wayyipqōd) from all over Israel, and "sent" word (וַיִּשְׁלַח, *wayyišlaḥ*)
to Jehoshaphat to invoke another round of covenantal prerogatives.
What is more, Jehoshaphat responds verbatim to Ahab's request when
he is asked to move against Ramoth-Gilead.

TABLE 7: Comparison of 1 Kings 22:4 and 2 Kings 3:7

1 Kings 22:4	2 Kings 3:7
I am as you. My people are as your people. My horses are as your horses.	I will go up. I am as you. My people are as your people. My horses are as your horses.
כָּמוֹנִי כָמוֹךָ כְּעַמְּךָ כְעַמֶּךָ כְּסוּסַי כְּסוּסֶיךָ	כָּמוֹנִי כָמוֹךָ כְּעַמְּךָ כְעַמֶּךָ כְּסוּסַי כְּסוּסֶיךָ
kāmônî kāmôkā kə'ammî kə'ammekā kəsûsay kəsûsêkā	*kāmônî kāmôkā kə'ammî kə'ammekā kəsûsay kəsûsêkā*

However, Jehoshaphat plays a more strategic role in 2 Kings 3
than in 1 Kings 22. According to 2 Kings 3:8, J(eh)oram yields to
Jehoshaphat's suggestion for what route to take: "[J(eh)oram] asked,
'Which way shall we go up?' [Jehoshaphat] answered, 'The wilderness road of Edom.'" Unfortunately, Jehoshaphat's advice proved to
be extremely problematic for the campaign.

Second Kings 3:9 recounts how the three-nation coalition fell into
peril. After seven days of advancing on Moabite territory by a route
that sought to exploit the vulnerable southern border, they arrived
at a position that offered no water: "So the king of Israel, the king of
Judah, and the king of Edom mobilized. They made a surrounding
approach that took seven days, but there was no water for the camp or

---

[Atlanta: SBL Press, 2003], 29, 55, 64; see also Philip J. King and Lawrence E. Stager, *Life in Biblical Israel*, Library of Ancient Israel [Louisville: Westminster John Knox, 2001], 113–14).

for the beasts which were with them."[6] The wilderness of Edom was treacherous, and the only hope for successful navigation was access to water sources and a keen awareness of where routes led.

In light of this, the Israelite king's lament makes sense (2 Kgs 3:10). Such an ignominious end to their campaign would have been deeply shameful and constituted a perceived indictment upon the leaders of the coalition. However, as in 1 Kings 22, Jehoshaphat requested prophetic guidance (2 Kgs 3:11): "Is there not a prophet of the Lord here, through whom we may inquire of the Lord?" Oddly, Elisha was ostensibly among the ranks of the army: "One of the servants of the king of Israel answered. He said, 'Elisha, son of Shaphat, who poured water over the hands of Elijah, is here.'" Jehoshaphat, in turn, led the other two kings to the prophet to inquire of Yahweh.

The coalition was received very coldly at first. Elisha essentially sent them away, angrily asking them why they did not just go to the prophets they normally consulted, their prophets of convenience. Nevertheless, the king of Israel interjects and appeals to divine approval (2 Kgs 3:13). Eventually Elisha reconsidered but made it clear that he obliged their request only because of Jehoshaphat. Without the influence of Jehoshaphat, Elisha would have ignored them altogether.

What follows (2 Kgs 3:15–19) is a window into the prophetic *modus operandi*.[7] The context assumed by the scene certainly classifies as a time of crisis, and the prophet is sought out for insight on how to proceed. Moreover, the text testifies that a prophetic utterance could be linked to a sudden onslaught of the Lord's power accompanied by other elements; here it was facilitated by music (3:15). Certainly not all prophetic encounters happened this way, but in this case it did. As for the message, it was both cryptic and definite. On the one

---

6. "The maneuver demonstrates an attempt to take the Moabites by surprise in a region where Moabite strength would be less consentrated" (Sweeney, *I & II Kings*, 281).

7. For a useful institutional profile, see Schreiner, *Pondering the Spade*, 30–34. See also the classic studies that still influence the conversation: Abraham Malamat, "Prophecy at Mari," in *The Place Is Too Small for Us: The Israelite Prophets in Recent Scholarship*, ed. Robert P. Gordon, Sources for Biblical and Theological Studies 5 (Winona Lake, IN: Eisenbrauns, 1995), 50–73; Moshe Weinfeld, "Ancient Near Eastern Patterns in Prophetic Literature," *VT* 27 (1977): 178–95.

FIGURE 9: **The topography around Arad—the Israelite coalition would have passed through this territory en route to Moab**

hand, the coalition would witness a mysterious rush of water when the wadi filled with pools of water. On the other hand, there would be no preparation for the event: "You will perceive no wind. You will see no rain. But this wadi will be filled with water so that you, your cattle, and your large animals will drink" (3:17). And, as if to preempt any statement of disbelief before it could be audibly processed by the audience, the second part of the oracle (3:18) shifted the focus to the outcome of the battle, predicting complete victory described by stock phrases associated with successful military campaigns: "He will give Moab into your hand. You will strike every fortified city and every choice city. Every good tree you will cut down, and you will stop up every source of water. And you will spoil all the good plots of land with stones." And right on cue, "at the time of the morning offering" (בַּעֲלוֹת הַמִּנְחָה, *kaʿălôt hamminḥâ*), without warning, water filled the wadi.

6.2 THE POTENTIAL LITERARY DEVELOPMENT OF 2 KINGS 3

This encounter between the kings and the prophet is an entertaining way to introduce the conflict with Moab. It is filled with social and personal rivalry, the mysterious and the miraculous, and the lasting legacies of certain people. Yet there is reason to wonder if this prophetic encounter is secondary to the account of Mesha's rebellion. Second Kings 3:8 closes with the phrase "the way of the wilderness of Edom" (דֶּרֶךְ מִדְבַּר אֱדוֹם, *derek midbar ʾĕdôm*). A similar phrase is repeated in 3:20 (מִדֶּרֶךְ אֱדוֹם, *midderek ʾĕdôm*), right before the phrase "the land was filled with water" (וַתִּמָּלֵא הָאָרֶץ אֶת־הַמָּיִם, *wattimmālēʾ hāʾāreṣ ʾet hammāyim*). If this repetition is understood as intentional resumption, then the original account of Mesha's rebellion spanned 3:4–8; 20b–27.[8] Such a proposal could explain the shift in characterization surrounding Jehoshaphat. In 3:4–8, the Judean king is passive and subordinate to the Israelite king, who is dictating terms and expectations. However, in 3:9–20a, Jehoshaphat confidently navigates the crisis by calling upon Elisha, and he is the reason why Elisha did not just walk away. In contrast, a secondary status for 3:9–20a could also explain the sudden appearance of Elisha.

However, this proposal would create an odd dynamic for the narrative, not to mention that the phrases incorporating "the way of Edom" are not identical. Nevertheless, assuming for the moment that *derek midbar ʾĕdôm* (2 Kgs 3:8) and *midbar ʾĕdôm* (3:20) mark the boundaries of the intercalation, then the original account at 3:8 and 3:20b would have read:

---

8. Erasmus Gass notes the association of *midbar ʾĕdôm* in this passage. However, his connections are more general and thematic. In the end, Gass sees an original account of 2 Kings 3:4–6 and 3:24–27 that was expanded by 3:7–23 (Erasmus Gass, "Topographical Considerations and Redaction Criticism in 2 Kings 3," *JBL* 128.1 [2009]: 81–84).

וַיֹּאמֶר אֵי־זֶה הַדֶּרֶךְ נַעֲלֶה וַיֹּאמֶר דֶּרֶךְ (מִדְבַּר) אֱדוֹם וַתִּמָּלֵא הָאָרֶץ
אֶת־הַמָּיִם

wayyō'mer 'ê-ze hadderek na'ăle wayyō'mer derek (midbar)
'ĕdôm wattimālē' hā'āreṣ 'et-hammāyim

He asked, "By which way shall we go?" He said, "The (wilderness) road of Edom." But the land was filled with water.

In such a reconstruction, the issues of chronology and the filling
of the land with water are issues that need to be addressed. Regarding
the former, the narrative would have moved very quickly. The coalition would have developed their strategy and then immediately found
themselves at the border of Moab facing their aquatic obstacle. In the
case of the latter, how did the land—the wilderness of Edom—get filled
with water? Consequently, if this reconstruction is accepted, the prophetic narrative of 3:9–20a may have been developed and inserted to
clarify the questions of chronology and the presence of water.

Nevertheless, suggesting that the resumption of the wilderness
road signals a later insertion appears to be a stretch. The phrases
in 2 Kings 3:8 and 3:20b are not precise enough.[9] Indeed, there are
lingering questions of characterization and the sudden appearance
and disappearance of Elisha, both of which demand an explanation,
but any argument for seeing 3:9–20a as a later insertion needs to be
made on other grounds.[10]

---

9. The imprecision could be indicative of conflation, indicating a potential editorial marker.
In this view, the initial phrase *derek midbar 'ĕdôm* was abbreviated to *midbar 'ĕdôm*, thereby
highlighting the boundaries of an insertion. Levinson notes this option and cites Tigay and
Fishbane in support (Levinson, *Hermeneutics of Innovation*, 143 n. 191; see also Jeffrey H. Tigay
"Conflation as a Redactional Technique," in *Empirical Models for Biblical Criticism*, ed. Jeffrey H.
Tigay [Philadelphia: University of Pennsylvania Press, 1985] 53–96; Michael Fishbane, *Biblical
Interpretation in Ancient Israel* [1988; repr., Oxford: Clarendon Press, 2004], 86 n. 20). This
possibility, in our estimation, remains unlikely.

10. Gass argues for an original narrative that was expanded, citing thematic and lexical
connections to other places in Kings, the presence of Jehoshaphat after his death notice in
1 Kings 22:51, and the fact that 22:24–27 only mention the Israelite force (Gass, "Topographical
Considerations," 81–84).

6.3 MOAB VERSUS THE
ISRAELITE COALITION

The actual account of the conflict begins in earnest at 2 Kings 3:21.
When Moab understands what is upon them, they leverage every
resource to marshal a defense. The text recounts that Moab's force
was "mustered from everyone who girds up for battle on up the
ranks" (וַיִּצָּעֲקוּ מִכֹּל חֹגֵר חֲגֹרָה וָמָעְלָה, *wayyēṣā'ăqû mikkōl ḥōgēr ḥagōrâ
wāma'ălâ*).[11] When they were prepared, the Moabite force mobilized
"at the border of" (עַל־הַגְּבוּל, *'al haggəbûl*) Moab and Edom, most
likely in the vicinity of the Zered Valley.[12] According to the biblical
account, the Moabite force arose in the morning to see "the water"
glimmering "red like blood" (הַמַּיִם אֲדֻמִּים כַּדָּם, *hammayim 'ădumîm
kaddām*), which was interpreted as a sign of infighting between the
Israelite, Judean, and Edomite coalition.[13] Thus, when the Moabite
force entered the camp, thinking to plunder it, they were terribly
wrong and a rout ensued (3:24): "Israel arose and struck Moab, and
they fled before them. Israel moved against them, attacking Moab."[14]
But the Israelite response did not end at the border of Moab and

---

11. The Hebrew is grammatically awkward: "And they were mustered from all the ones
girding a girdle and above." The language suggests that the Moabite troops were marshalled from
any man old enough to properly wear garments for war, which would include men incapable of
garnishing a sword for battle. It also suggests an all-hands-on-deck approach to the battle, from
infantry, to archer, to cavalry, and charioteer. Another possibility could read: "mustered from
everyone who girds up for battle and lifts the weapon." However, this interpretation requires
the verbal idea "to lift" from the adverb *maǎlâ* ("upward"), which is problematic.

12. Rasmussen, *Zondervan Atlas*, 61–62.

13. In 2 Kings 3:20 the water flowed from "Edom" (*'ĕdôm*), while in 3:22 the water flowed
"red" (*'ădumîm*) as blood. We understand the play on words between "Edom" and "red" as
heightening the contrast between Israel's two Transjordanian vassals. Whereas Moab had
rebelled against Israel by withholding tribute, Edom demonstrated its allegiance by fighting
alongside Judah. Judah's status as a vassal seems clear based on the covenant language in 3:7
("your people are my people, my horses are your horses"), but also from Joash's identification
as "the Samarian" in the Tell Rimah Stela of Adad-nirari III (see Greenwood, "Late Tenth- and
Ninth-Century Issues," 301).

14. The MT is corrupt, signified by the *ketiv/qere*. The Masoretes suggest reading *wayyakkû
bāh* (וַיַּכּוּ־בָהּ), which has support in some manuscript and Targumic traditions. However, the
LXX tradition is apparently reading a form of *bw'* (בוא), which we follow, although it assumes
an abnormal (but not unprecedented) orthography (see Mordechai Cogan and Hayim Tadmor,
II Kings, AB 11 [New Haven: Yale University Press, 1988], 45).

Edom. Rather, the Israelites and its contingent pursued the Moabites and ravaged their land as they went (3:25): "Now the cities, they tore down. On every good parcel of land, each man threw his stone and they filled it. All the sources of water, they stopped up. Every good tree they cut down." The rout continued all the way to Kir-hareseth. But even there, slingers surrounded the fortified city and bombarded it with projectiles (3:25).

What happened at Kir-hareseth remains one of the most perplexing events in Israelite history (2 Kgs 3:26–27):

> When the king of Moab saw that the battle was too strong from him, he took with him 700 men with drawn swords to break through the king of Edom. But they were not able. Then he took his son, who would rule after him, and presented him as a sacrifice upon the wall. Then a great anger came upon Israel. Then they departed from it and returned to the land.

To begin, it is not clear where Kir-hareseth should be located, although many scholars believe that it aligns with modern day Kerak.[15] If this is correct, then its strategic value for Moab goes without saying: Kir-hareseth was then located at the intersection of the King's Highway and other important east-west trade routes. At the top of a plateau, Kerak later became home to a famous Crusader castle. However, the difficulty of the passage is also linked to understanding what actually happened. According to the simplest reading of the text, when the Moabite king realized that defeat was at hand, he sacrificed his heir, which somehow incurred a great wrath upon Israel. In turn, Israel abruptly left the besieged city. This is, unfortunately, less than clear. In addition, there is the frustrating cliff-hanger that remains at

---

15. The LXX translates "Kir" (קִיר, *qîr*) as *tou teichous* (τοῦ τείχους), "wall," suggesting the "wall(s) of Haraseth." An important passage appears in Isaiah 16:17, which lists several Moabite towns in the context of a judgment oracle. There, *qîr ḥărāśet* (קִיר־חֲרָשֶׂת) appears (Gerald Mattingly, "Kir-Hareseth," *ABD* 4:84). However, as we will see below, this is by no means definitive. The identification of Kir-hareseth is a critical consideration when pondering the historicity of the biblical account.

the end of the scene. Was Moab brought back in line as a vassal? Or did their rebellion persist? What happened on the top of that wall? Whose wrath actually fell upon Israel?

Commentary on this scene is wide ranging across the history of scholarship. From Josephus to Rabbi Qimhi, from nineteenth century scholars to the present day, ideas have ranged from a temporary pause in besiegement to an utter failure.[16] In the extreme case of Mordechai Cogan and Hayim Tadmor, they believe that the ambiguity inherent to the scene can only be explained as "an embarrassment" that stems from a perceived unfulfilled prophecy.[17] Yet Drew Holland has recently proposed another way forward.[18] Instead of existing as some type of commentary on a failed prophecy, as the expression of Chemosh's anger, or as punishment for ignoring the divine mandated expectations of war (see Deut 20), this scene functions as another indictment against Omride policy. According to Holland, Elijah's prophecy is indeed fulfilled.[19] Not only do 2 Kings 3:19 and 3:25 collaborate to suggest a victory for the Israelite coalition, but the notification of 3:26 also appears to support such a victory. Why would the king of Moab seek to break the siege if not for the perception that victory was effectively lost? But more importantly, Holland argues that the sacrifice of the Moabite prince should not be understood as some primal effort to appease the wrath of Chemosh in the hope of a miraculous victory.[20] Rather, based on the biblical evidence, the ʿōlâ (עֹלָה) offered here should be understood apologetically, as a sacrifice of contrition offered immediately after conflict by a rebellious

---

16. For a useful summary, see Drew S. Holland, "An Alternative Approach to the Dilemma of 2 Kgs 3:27," *Journal of Inductive Biblical Studies* 7.2 (2020): 7–8.

17. Cogan and Tadmor, *II Kings*, 51.

18. What follows is a summary of Holland's argument (Holland, "Alternative Approach," 7–31).

19. In contrast, Sweeney argues that the wrath that fell upon Israel was not punitive but rather an anger born out of the shocking scenario they witnessed. Thus, the oracle failed because J(eh)oram and his coalition failed to see victory through (Sweeney, *I & II Kings*, 284).

20. According to Holland, this perspective is the dominant understanding of the sacrifice (see Holland, "Alternative Approach," 14–15 n. 15).

vassal.[21] Such a scenario also explains the sacrifice of the firstborn. It was not a gruesome, primal practice, but a substitutionary, practical, and psychological offering. With the death of the Moabite prince, not only would the possibility of intergenerational rebellion be drastically reduced, but the rebellious scandal would have haunted Mesha for the rest of his life.[22]

Regarding the wrath that descended upon Israel, Holland rightly acknowledges the textual ambiguity. However, he emphasizes that it is not random or arbitrary: "It functions to indicate that the Israelites were behaving in a culturally ambiguous, thus inappropriate manner."[23] Moreover, Holland contends that the ambiguity is linked to the history between Israel and Moab. Whether through a religious, social, or military convergence, the histories of Moab and Israel were intertwined. By implication, according to Holland, the recipient of Mesha's sacrifice was not strictly Chemosh. And even if the Moabites and Israelites had their respective gods in mind while sacrificing, the net result of their deed was a worshipful action directed to an unknown god. According to Holland, the text reflects this syncretistic situation through its lack of clarity.[24] It then follows that the wrath that descended upon Israel is indeed Yahwistic, caused by their partaking in an inappropriate sacrifice that was at the center of an attempt to repair a fractured political relationship.

The strength of Holland's argument revolves around his explanation of the sacrifice offered by Mesha. The sacrifice is specific, an ʿōlâ, and what one observes in 2 Kings 3 matches the "pattern" of the ʿōlâ, whether in the ancient Near East or the context of ancient Israel. Moreover, the association of such a contrite sacrifice with contexts of covenantal infidelity is particularly astute. Thus, Holland is right

---

21. Holland bolsters this connection by establishing an analogy between 2 Kings 3 and the situation between King Ahaz and Tiglath-pileser III (see 2 Kgs 16).

22. Holland offers supporting passages (Gen 22; 2 Sam 12; Judg 11; and others; Holland, "Alternative Approach," 18–22).

23. Holland, "Alternative Approach," 23.

24. Holland, "Alternative Approach," 25.

to emphasize that Mesha's sacrifice is not an appeal to Chemosh for some miraculous victory from the jaws of defeat. Rather, it is more precisely understood as a sacrifice offered in response to a rebellion that demanded steep retribution. Nevertheless, Holland's argument for the subsequent wrath as Yahwistic is stretched regarding his presumption of syncretism, which is constructed only on general historical connections. Regardless, our contention is that the anger is Yahwistic, although we come to that conclusion from a different angle.

The major point for this study is that Mesha's offering of an apologetic sacrifice implies that the Israelite force was attempting to reconcile the fractured political relationship and such a posture would have conflicted with the prophetic prognostication of complete victory (2 Kgs 3:18–19). The scene describes the Israelite force as—once again—prioritizing political relationships over obedience to Yahweh and his desires. This is what incurs the wrath of Yahweh. Moreover, this is remarkably similar to the errors of Ahab at the end of 1 Kings 20, and further contributes to the pattern that persists throughout the historical record.

6.4 THE MOABITE STONE
AND ITS TESTIMONY

The Moabite Stone, or Mesha Stele, also speaks to the events of 2 Kings 3 but contextualizes them in a larger celebration of the Moabite king and Moab's national deity. As such, it is another extrabiblical voice that is vital for understanding the dynamics of the Omride conflicts.

In 1868, F. A. Klein was traversing the Transjordanian plateau with the intention of serving the local Arab populations.[25] Eventually, his journeys took him to a local Bedouin population near modern day Dhibon, where he learned of a nearby inscription. When he saw the large basalt stele, he rightly understood that the thirty-four lines of text were significant and proceeded to sketch the stele, copy

---

25. This description of the stele's fate summarizes the account offered by Siegfried H. Horn, "Why the Moabite Stone was Blown to Pieces," *BAR* 12.3 (1986): 30–37.

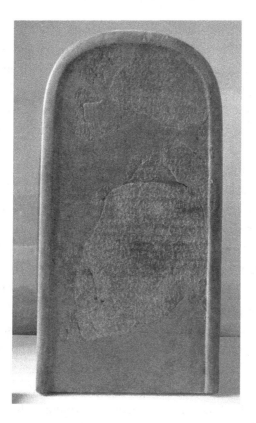

FIGURE 10: **The Moabite Stone**

a few letters for reference, and negotiate an initial purchase price of approximately $400.

Klein then returned to Jerusalem where he contacted German authorities. J. Heinrich Petermann obtained approval from his German superiors and then engaged local customs to secure the stele. They were unfortunately compromised by local rivalries and economic ambition, raising the initial price of $400 to roughly $4,000. Naturally, this produced another round of negotiations, which eventually settled at about $480. However, nearby tribes prohibited the transport of the stele through their territory, a turn of events that severely frustrated Petermann.

About a year after Klein's discovery, Charles Clermont-Ganneau entered the equation. He dispatched a friend to try and procure the stele and during the second visitation, Ganneau's confidant was able to produce a papier-mâché impression of the stele that later proved critical to its translation. According to the account, a fight among local groups broke out, threatening Ganneau's man with mortal danger. He escaped to Jerusalem with the torn papier-mâché impression in his possession. Concurrent with these events, the Germans persuaded the Turkish authorities to send troops to forcibly remove the stele from the possession of the fighting Bedouins. In response, the Bedouins shattered the stele into pieces and distributed them throughout the region. It goes without saying that such a destructive action was demoralizing. Nevertheless, Ganneau, enlisting the aid of Charles Warren, endeavored to procure as many pieces of the original inscription as possible. They were eventually able to gather enough pieces that, with the help of the original papier-mâché squeeze, the stele could be reconstructed with a significant level of precision.

The stele, before it was shattered, stood almost four feet tall. Containing almost forty lines of text written in Moabite—a Northwest Semitic dialect—it recounts the historical exploits of King Mesha of Moab.[26] It is dedicated to the Moabite god Chemosh for his role in saving Mesha and Moab from their enemies (lines 3–4) and is specifically recounted in terms of Moab's revolt against Israel. According to the stele, Omride oppression was "because Chemosh was angry against the land" (בי יאנף כמש בארצה, *ky y'np kmš b'rsh*). Yet Chemosh's anger eventually waned, and the god returned the land to Mesha and Moab. And it was because of this restoration that Mesha embarked on a nation-wide campaign that not only saw the reallocation of

---

26. Moabite displays many linguistic affinities with epigraphic Hebrew. Among the most important linguistic elements are the contraction of diphthongs, the so-called Canaanite Shift, the presence of the *wayyiqtol* form, the direct object marker *'ēt* (אֶת), the definite article as *heh* (ה), and the relative *'ašer* (אֲשֶׁר). For a detailed description of Moabite, particularly its relationship to epigraphic Hebrew, see Peter Bekins, *Inscriptions from the World of the Bible: A Reader and Introduction to Old Northwest Semitic* (Peabody, MA: Hendrickson Academic, 2020), 3–46; 147; Garr, *Dialect Geography of Syria-Palestine*.

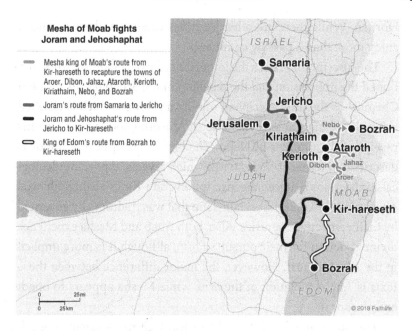

MAP 6: **Mesha of Moab fights Joram and Jehoshaphat**

---

territories traditionally held by Moab but also the refortification of
these locations.

The structure of the inscription is three-fold. The first section, line
1 through the first portion of line 3, should be understood as the introduction that explains the benefactor, the benefactor's lineage, and the
function of the memorial. The second portion of line 3 through line
8 appear to be a type of historical prologue, which recounts Moab's
vassalship under Ahab and that his successors "oppressed Moab for
a lengthy period" (ויענו את מאב ימן רבן, wyʿnw ʾt mʾb ymn rbn). Most
interestingly, vassalship to Israel is presented as divine punishment,
which is reminiscent of Judges and its theological framework rooted
in divine retribution.

The final section of the inscription is by far the longest. It recounts
numerous military encounters and reconstruction efforts that were
linked to Mesha's pursuit of freedom (lines 9–34). Yet within the
final section, the focus falls upon Ataroth, Nebo, Yahaz, Qarhoh, and

Hornen. While there are other locations cataloged, these locations enjoy more than a passing comment.

The inscription praises the important role of Chemosh, who sanctioned the oppression *and* the rebellion of the Moabites. In addition, Chemosh is the direct recipient of military honor, which is clarified not only by his stated ownership of Ataroth (line 12) but also his receipt of the plunder of Nebo. The latter description of honor is described in terms of *ḥrm* (חרם), which reveals important ideological connections between the inscription and 1 Kings 20. In both texts, Ahab and Mesha seek to reclaim land that was traditionally governed by their respective countries. Also, both Ahab and Mesha experience divine sanction for their pursuit of *ḥrm*, although it is more implicit in the Moabite text. However, the major difference between these texts is Ahab's violation of the *ḥrm*, while Mesha appears to obediently honor it.

The question of each text's historical legitimacy remains of critical importance. The situation between 2 Kings 3 and the Moabite Stone is similar to the one entertained in the second chapter of this work regarding the Tel Dan Stele and 2 Kings 9–10. Do they exhibit an "either/or" situation, where one is compelled to determine whether the Moabite or the biblical account enjoys historical value while the other does not? Philip Stern argues that the biblical account is so ideologically slanted that it is largely useless at the historical level.[27] He suggests that its chronological difficulties and its poetics establish it as a problematic historical source.[28] With respect to the issue of historiographic poetics, Stern emphasizes that Mesha, king of Moab, is a passive character in the biblical tradition, which ostensibly contrasts with the active characterization of the stele. Also, the biblical

---

27. Philip Stern, "Of Kings and Moabites: History and Theology in 2 Kings 3 and the Mesha Inscription," *HUCA* 64 (1993): 1–14; Stern, *The Biblical Herem: A Window into Israel's Religious Experience*, Brown Judaic Studies (Atlanta: Scholars Press, 2020), 50–54.

28. The chronological issues that Stern cites arise from the Greek textual tradition and center on Elijah and J(eh)oram. As we have discussed above, these chronological difficulties defy explanation.

presentation is influenced by its Judean point of view and an obvious concern for the prophetic office. Finally, Stern invokes Erasmus Gass's study that highlights the topographical difficulties in 2 Kings 3.[29] Joe Sprinkle adds other complications, from the size of Moab's tribute, to the presence of Elisha in the camp, to the comical portrayal of the Israelite coalition's military strategy.[30] Together, these observations are often marshalled when framing 2 Kings 3 as a highly idealized account.

On the one hand, Stern and those like him rightly note the poetic intricacies of the biblical presentation. It presents a concern for prophetic activity in the geo-politics of that era, as well as reflecting a Judean point of view. Moreover, the chronological difficulties of Omride succession vis-à-vis their Judean counterparts are incontrovertible and the notification of Jehoshaphat's death notice in 1 Kings 22:51 demands attention. On the other hand, Stern's analysis fails to properly consider the historiographic dynamics of the Moabite text, particularly as a memorial inscription, where the active characterization of Mesha is consistent with its literary conventions. These realizations about the genre and literary conventions actually militate against Stern's statement that "Mesha could not have left such an account of his accomplishments if he were the Moabite equivalent to Hezekiah after Sennacherib."[31] Stern is referring to the general notion that Hezekiah's account of Sennacherib's siege of Jerusalem was recounted in response to the socio-economic devastation that followed his rebellion and defiance: Hezekiah sanctioned the account of Jerusalem's siege in a way to save face. However, we believe that a similar function underlies the stele—as well as 2 Kings 3 for that matter. Both presentations likely sought to present the events of Moab's rebellion in a way that angled its audience away from certain historical realities and promoted a specific message. The historical task, therefore, is to examine each presentation in a way that accommodates such

29. Gass, "Topographical Considerations," 65–84.

30. Joe M. Sprinkle, "2 Kings 3: History of Historical Fiction?" *BBR* 9 (1999): 253–54.

31. Stern, *Biblical Herem*, 51.

a realization. Of course, this is only effectively accomplished if we accept that the biblical account contains historical value and can be synthesized with Mesha's presentation.

Joe Sprinkle has offered such a synthesis. He begins by constructing a historical framework by considering the testimonies of both the Judean and Moabite presentations.[32]

1. Mesha was the king of Moab

2. Mesha was a vassal to the Omride dynasty

3. Israel's God was Yahweh while Moab's god was Chemosh

4. When Mesha rebelled, he asserted independence from Israel

5. Mesha was in charge of a large-scale herding operation

6. Mesha was willing to kill for religious reasons

7. Mesha was convinced that Chemosh drove away his enemies

8. The tribe of Gad occupied disputed territory with the Moabites north of the Arnon

9. Mesha conducted a military campaign south of the Arnon

10. Mesha's southern campaign explains Edom's role in the conflict

For Sprinkle, this framework is foundational: "Since the biblical text appears true to life in some details, one cannot quickly dismiss the possibility of accurate details not subject to verification by external sources or difficult to reconcile with external sources."[33] Sprinkle believes that one cannot dismiss the biblical witness out of hand,

---

32. See Sprinkle, "2 Kings 3," 254–57.
33. Sprinkle, "2 Kings 3," 257.

although proponents of the biblical witness's historical veracity must properly address the issues brought up by Stern and those like him. Nevetheless, arguments that question the legitimacy of an Edomite king in 2 Kings 3 are tempered by a tendency to discuss Edomite kingship imprecisely and inconsistently.[34] Also, the chronological difficulties are eased when one realizes the schematic range of terms like "son" and "years" in certain genres.[35] Regarding the apparent geographic difficulties in the biblical account, the traditional identification of Kirhareseth with modern day Kerak is less than definitive. And if Kirhareseth can be identified with a site in northern Moab, as some have postulated, then the length of the Israelite journey becomes "plausible rather than absurd."[36] Finally, the diachronic history of 2 Kings 3, or the fact that the biblical account is sometimes artistically flamboyant in nature, does not preclude its historical value. What ultimately matters, according to Sprinkle, is that each witness is "analyzed with the purposes of each text in mind."[37] Indeed, we concur that this method is the way forward.

6.5 CONCLUSIONS

Ultimately, one must accept that "the Mesha Inscription, like most royal inscriptions from ancient times, served as a piece of propaganda to glorify the king rather than a sober, objective historical account of what happened."[38] We have argued that the biblical account zeroes in on a particular event because of its value in bringing and reinforcing a sustained criticism of Omride policy. Consequently, the cumulative witness of 1 Kings 20, 22, and 2 Kings 3 demonstrates that Omride military practice often conflicted with Yahwistic religious values. Such policies valued political expedience over obedience to Yahweh's commands. By implication, therefore, the witnesses of the Mesha Stele

---

34. Consider 1 Kings 22:48 vis-à-vis 2 Kings 8:20.
35. *HALOT* 1:137–38; 2:1600–1601.
36. Sprinkle, "2 Kings 3," 260.
37. Sprinkle, "2 Kings 3," 265.
38. Sprinkle, "2 Kings 3," 265.

and 2 Kings 3 do not create an "either/or" proposition, where one
must determine the historical value of one witness at the expense of
the other. Rather, each witness has a role to play in reconstructing
the events and, by implication, understanding the message of the
biblical account. The key is to analyze each witness in light of its
own intentions.

But perhaps the final point is the most fascinating. The Moabite
Stone vis-à-vis the biblical witness appears to be similar to 2 Kings
9–10 and the Tel Dan Stele. Together, they testify to the diverse machinations that bore upon the history of the Omride dynasty, and each
witness presents that history in a way that suits its own sophisticated
historiographic purposes.

Chapter 7

CONCLUSIONS AND REFLECTIONS ON THE OMRIDE WARS AND BIBLICAL HISTORIOGRAPHY

The portrayal of conflict between Israel and Aram does not necessarily conflict with the portrayal of the alliance between Israel and Aram against Shalmaneser III at Qarqar.[1]

—Marvin Sweeney

This study has examined the Omride wars in detail, not only focusing on the biblical presentation of the dynasty's conflicts with the Arameans and Moabites but also the extrabiblical witnesses that attest to these international relations. Many reasons for this endeavor could be articulated, from personal academic interests to the Christian traditions and institutions that we have associated with in the past and in the present. However, the most important reason is that the accounts of the Omride wars have been historically undervalued in discussions of the dynamics of biblical historiography in general and of the Omride dynasty specifically. The Omrides are villainized

---

1. Sweeney, *I & II Kings*, 240.

unlike any other family across ancient Israel's historical literature. They are presented as the embodiment of everything wrong with the monarchal institution: its propensity to compromise theologically, to antagonize and reject the prophets of Yahweh, and to make unjust and selfish decisions at the expense of the larger society. Yet whereas the biblical witness regarding the Omride dynasty is overwhelmingly negative, the extrabiblical witnesses are rather positive.

Whether they are remembered as the dynastic foundation for the nation of Israel, or as the inspiration for Israelite culture during Iron II, the witnesses of Assyria and of archaeology speak to a resourceful and ambitious dynasty that set a positive course for Israel's cultural and geopolitical advancement. Thus, the well-informed reader of Scripture is inevitably faced with a challenging situation. Which perspective is correct? The biblical perspective, or the non-biblical perspective? History has shown this challenge as particularly difficult for certain traditions. But is such a polarizing choice the best course of action? Should it be an "either/or" proposition?

It has been our intention to show how the biblical and non-biblical testimonies surrounding this family do not have to be understood as antagonistic or be held in tension with one another, as if one must choose one group of testimonies at the expense of the other. Rather, the biblical and non-biblical witnesses supplement each other. Perhaps we can now say that they *need* each other. We have argued that the nature of historiography, or history writing—particularly ancient historiography—is intentionally sophisticated. Indeed, good history writing desires to articulate what happened in the past. Thus, it has an antiquarian interest. Yet accompanying this desire to articulate what happened is a desire to communicate something beyond events and persons. This means then that all history writing has an ideological agenda. By implication therefore, proper history writing, history writing that is faithful to the essence of what it tries to do, holds a balance. And the historian is tasked with determining how far the pendulum between antiquarian and systematic interests swings.[2] We believe that examining the biblical testimony of the Omride wars in concert with the relevant extrabiblical witnesses allows us to detect how far this pendulum swings with a greater degree of precision.

Perhaps another image is useful to explain our point: the seesaw. A seesaw needs weight at both ends to function. Now the weight does not need to be perfectly distributed for the seesaw to function, but it works most efficiently when the weight is comparable. However, if the weight disproportion is too extreme or non-existent, where most or all the weight is on one side, then the seesaw cannot function. Likewise, we maintain that proper history writing is not possible if there is too much concern, or sole concern, for either antiquarian interests or systematic interests. If a purported historical text is too concerned with an ideological interest or telling the audience mechanically what happened at the expense of any other point of emphasis, we question its validity as a historical text.

But again, the critical dynamic is that an antiquarian concern is present with a systematic one, at least to the point that they are both discernable. There is a balance that has to be struck between an account of what actually happened and whatever ideological point the writer wants to communicate. Indeed, some historical texts can be more systematic than others. Likewise, some historical texts can be more antiquarian than others. There is no better example of this than a comparison between Samuel/Kings and Chronicles.[3] Applied to the task of the Omride wars, it is clear to us that the biblical

---

2. On antiquarian and systematic interests, see section 2.2, page 17.

3. Both texts cover the same period of Israel's history, but they both do so with different emphases. For a useful primer on these dynamics, see Ronald K. Duke, "Chronicles, Book of," in *Dictionary of the Old Testament: Historical Books*, ed. Bill T. Arnold and H. G. M. Williamson (Downers Grove, IL: InterVarsity, 2005), 171–79. Most obviously, Chronicles does not recall many of the negative experiences recounted in 2 Samuel. Also, the Chronicler does not focus on the exploits of the northern kings, rather discussing them only in the context of a focus on Judean kings. Such a tendency illuminates how biblical historians perform on a spectrum that considers systematic and antiquarian interests in varying degrees.

presentation is not a fabrication, nor is it likely pulling events from a later period for the sake of some anti-Omride agenda. Rather, it is taking creative but widely accepted liberties in its historical presentation to ensure that a particular message is understood about the family. In terms of the seesaw analogy, it is off-balanced and leaning toward the systematic end of the spectrum. Moreover, this imbalance is precisely why we need the extrabiblical witnesses. They allow us to understand the systematic intentions of the Omride presentation more fully. Without the Assyrian, Moabite, and Aramean records, or even the archaeological record of Israel during the ninth and eighth centuries, we cannot fully appreciate the theological convictions of the biblical presentation.

After summarizing the historical context of the Omrides in chapter 1, chapter 2 opened the study proper by discussing the Tel Dan Stele in conjunction with 2 Kings 9–10, asking what could be determined about how the Omride dynasty finally met its demise. We suggested that the Aramaic and Hebrew texts are not inherently antagonistic. Rather, reading both texts in light of their literary intentions, one observes a deliberate attempt to present the turn of events in a way that efficiently communicates a particular point. With respect to the biblical text, the intended message is further affected by an intentional refinement to accommodate the prophetic role in the dynasty's demise. Based on the cumulative testimony, the downfall of the Omrides was ultimately the result of several machinations interacting with one another.

In pursuit of the question about the dynasty's demise, chapter 2 also articulated our method of investigation. Fundamentally, we committed to taking each witness as a serious voice in historical reconstruction. We also explained that such commitment is not naïve but reads critically, with attention to nuance, linguistic ambiguity, and literary convention. Similarly, we recognized that consulting inscriptions yields uncertain or tentative results in some instances. We also demonstrated that language can be elusive, that there may be more than meets the eye with certain claims. We readily observed that the biblical witnesses have the possibility of a long history of composition and development. Therefore, we concluded that there is no cookie-cutter mold that can be universally applied in hopes of accurate historical reconstruction. Rather, one's method must be malleable in light of the unique dynamics of each situation.

The third chapter engaged the first twenty-two verses of 1 Kings 20. The Aramean siege of Samaria was recounted, and by looking at the literary characterization of major characters, battle strategy, and prophetic involvement, we emphasized Israel's stunning victory. In addition, we pondered the history of Israelite and Aramean relations, concluding that they were particularly sour during the Iron Age, likely because both polities sought to exploit the same socio-political opportunities of the era.

Most importantly, however, we discussed at length the literary function of anonymity throughout 1 Kings 20. In many ways, this discussion is foundational to the conclusions of this study. We acknowledged that the tendency in the biblical text to use *melek* and *melek yiśrā'ēl* in a very pronounced manner has long been recognized. However, whereas many scholars interpret this phenomenon as evidence for a complex redactional program, we interpret it as historiographic convention, though we do not reject historical-critical possibilities in 1 Kings 20. Since anonymization appears throughout Israel's historical literature—and elsewhere in the ancient Near Eastern literary catalog—we interpret the data differently. This anonymization has the effect of relegating specific people beneath an institution so that institution can be critiqued against and compared to other institutions. In the case of the Omride dynasty, this anonymization functioned to highlight values that defined the dynasty's policies of conflict and positioned them in opposition to certain realities of Israelite society and theology.

Chapter 4 discussed the battle of Aphek as a sequel to the siege of Samaria. Clearly linked to 1 Kings 20:1–22, 20:23–34 documents what happened when Ben-Hadad sought to redeem his tragic loss a season earlier. Unfortunately, he and his coalition once again suffered

a humiliating defeat. This chapter also examined in detail the description of the Israelite army given in 20:27. Often understood as a phrase
denoting a diminutive and weak force, 20:27 is often marshalled as
evidence in the proposal that 1 Kings 20 and 22 were original to a
later period of Israel's history and later applied to Ahab for ideological reasons. We argued that the traditional understanding of 20:27
is off the mark. Instead, the image suggests an agitated army, ready
to fight, although vastly outnumbered. We proposed that this image
aligns better with what is known about the military capabilities of
the Omride dynasty.

But most importantly for chapter 4, we argued that the Israelite
king's critical error was to seek a political renegotiation with the
defeated Aramean king, rather than take him out of the geopolitical situation. In doing so, Israel violated the *ḥērem* placed upon the
Aramean king, and instead created a puppet king shackled by the
expectations of a newly negotiated treaty.

Chapter 5 shifts scenes from the battle at Aphek to the battle of
Ramoth-Gilead. Representing the natural progression from 1 Kings 20,
1 Kings 22 effectively articulates how the Israelite king's recently
assumed *ḥērem* status plays out. Thus, we argued that 1 Kings 22
echoes 1 Kings 20 in many ways. Nevertheless, we observed differences between the chapters, where the most important one is Israel
as the aggressor. Moreover, the theater of war around Ramoth-Gilead
is difficult to identify locationally, although the difficulty is overcome
by a clear and entertaining battle account. After insisting that a legitimate prophet of Yahweh be consulted on the eve of battle, Jehoshaphat
assumed a role on the battlefield as a decoy. Yet when the intensity of
the battle reached its apex and bore directly upon him, Jehoshaphat's
primal urges took over. He bailed on his duty, confessed his identity,
and fled as Ahab was left mortally wounded.

We proposed that the historical difficulties surrounding this battle
can be explained historiographically. On the one hand, the tension
involving a later conflict at Ramoth-Gilead (see 2 Kgs 8:28–29) can
be explained by the expansion of the historical record to include a

prophetic mechanism in the demise of the Omride family. This like-lihood demonstrates that the battle of Ramoth-Gilead became ideal for theological commentary. In turn, we proposed that this may shed further light on the anonymity characterizing 1 Kings 22. It is more than a literary convention relegating people to offices for the sake of dynastic criticism. It is also a mechanism to connect the Golden Age of the Omrides with the moment of its demise. The king most responsible for the dynasty's successes also planted the seeds of its fall.

The sixth chapter of our investigation stands apart from the previous chapters. We observed that the recounting of Moab's rebellion in 2 Kings 3 is not as closely tied together as 1 Kings 20 is with 1 Kings 22 through literary sequencing and historical progression. However, its characters, such as Jehoshaphat or an Omride king like Ahab or Je(ho)ram, the phenomenon of general anonymization, and certain characterizations do connect 2 Kings 3 with 1 Kings 20 and 22 under the umbrella of the Omride wars. Most importantly, 2 Kings 3 shares their concern for criticizing Omride wartime policies.

We noted that 2 Kings 3:1–3 functions as the introduction for the account, and J(eh)oram is presented as a more moderate, but still flawed, Omride king. This general characterization is then particularized in the account that follows. He still desired to leverage political possibilities against obedience to Yahweh, and he did not hesitate to invoke covenantal prerogatives to marshal a coalition and reclaim Israelite territory. However, he appears less dominant and decisive than the Omride king in 1 Kings 20 and 22. He absorbed prophetic chastisement and was technically the leader of the coalition that abandoned a siege at its apparent moment of victory. Yet he allowed Jehoshaphat to dictate the route to Moab. Most importantly, 2 Kings 3 continues the criticism of military policy established in 1 Kings 20 and 22. We proposed this based on an incorporation of recent research on the nature of the sacrifice offered on the walls of Kir-hareseth.

We consulted the Moabite account of Israel's conflicts with Moab in order to clarify the systematic tendency of the biblical account. The divergences between the biblical material and the Moabite Stone demonstrate that J(eh)oram's conflict with Moab represents another example of problematic military policies, policies that pitted the Omride family against the will of Yahweh. We concluded that the value of the Moabite Stone resides, at least partially, in its ability to clarify the historiographic qualities of the biblical record.

It is worth repeating, particularly since so much of contemporary scholarship is entrenched in the position that the Omride wars are accounts actualized from later periods in Israel's history, that we do not reject the idea that the accounts of the Omride dynasty, particularly their wars, were expanded through time. Neither do we reject the possibility that such developments were extensive and in accord with prophetic criticism. What we do reject is the notion that the accounts of the Omride wars are a transplant from a later period. We believe that much of the data historically marshalled to make this argument should be interpreted differently. Front and center is the tendency to speak of many royal characters in generalized institutional terms. It is reasonable to see this phenomenon as a literary convention employed to relegate personalities to the institution they represent for the purpose of a sustained criticism of dynastic policy. It also functions as a trigger to alert the audience to literary conventions within the presentation.

At this point, it is prudent to acknowledge a recent publication by Cat Quine as our conclusions display significant overlap with her investigation of 1 Kings 20 and 22. In "Victory as Defeat," Quine argues that the presentation of Ahab in 1 Kings 20 intentionally inflates Ahab in order to tear him down.[4] Quine writes, "I Kgs 20 is a literary composition designed to raise Ahab up as an exemplar of a strong Yahwistic king with an aim of subversively undermining him and the Omride dynasty that he represents."[5] Here, Quine privileges the literary questions of 1 Kings 20 and 22 over historical ones. Consequently,

---

4. Cat Quine, "Victory as Defeat: Narrative Subversion of Omride Strength in 1 Kings 20," *JTS* (2021): 1–14, DOI: 10.1093/jts/flabo61. This article was published after our manuscript was submitted, too late to be fully integrated into our study.

5. Quine, "Victory as Defeat," 3.

"although we could look for identifiable historical data in I Kgs 20, therefore, the question is, are we supposed to? The number of literary features and the connections with other parts of the biblical text seem to suggest a negative response—I Kgs 20 is a narrative talking about history rather than objectively reporting history itself."[6]

In making her argument, she astutely describes important literary mechanisms in 1 Kings 20, including the motif of seeking the council of elders prior to any military engagement. The result is an intriguing construction of Ahab as a paradigmatic and ideal king. Yet Quine emphasizes that such a characterization sets up the dramatic fall. Thus, the prophetic critique of 1 Kings 20:35–43 is the climax of the chapter and pivotal to the entire presentation: "Ahab is raised up *so that* he can be undermined to greater effect."[7]

Quine's study exhibits many points of contact with our conclusions. She recognizes the incontrovertible connections between 1 Kings 20 and 22, even arguing that both cooperate to achieve a common objective. Quine also emphasizes the importance of the prophetic critique in this program. And, perhaps most importantly, she agrees that the person of Ahab represents more than himself. Nevertheless, our study also diverges in important ways. First, our study connects 1 Kings 20 and 22 with 2 Kings 3, effectively expanding the scope of the dynastic critique. And while Quine ultimately suggests a "didactic function" for 1 Kings 20 and 22, that kingship is about more than military effectiveness, our focus upon the violation of the ḥērem establishes a more pointed criticism of the Omride dynasty.

Most importantly, our study diverges from Quine's in that the anonymization of the Israelite king is understood in a larger context, both biblically and historically. In turn, our study engages the historical problems of the Omride campaigns in greater details. The result, therefore, is a study that engages the convergence of the historical and literary dynamics at the heart of ancient historiography.

---

6. Quine, "Victory as Defeat," 7.

7. Quine, "Victory as Defeat," 11, emphasis original.

Before, concluding, we must entertain the context in which our proposed criticism of the Omride dynasty may have been produced. Or, to put it another way, what was the purpose and intention behind the critique's formulation and development? Dominic Rudman argues that the Rabshakeh's monologue during the siege of Jerusalem in 701 BC highlights the choice that Hezekiah faced.[8] According to Rudman, the Rabshakeh's speech is "full of prophetisms."[9] From its location (see 1 Kgs 18:17), echoing Isaiah's words to Ahaz (see Isa 7:5), to its content in conjunction with the Rabshakeh's social function as a royal ambassador, the Rabshakeh should be understood as an "anti-Isaiah."[10] Moreover, the issue that both Isaiah and the Rabshakeh present to Hezekiah regards who the king should trust. On the one hand, Hezekiah can continue to embrace what the Rabshakeh describes as deceptive trust in the conviction that Judah will be saved. On the other hand, Hezekiah could reject the hope of Yahweh and trust that Assyria will lead Judah in a new exodus, to a new land defined by plenty and safety. Rudman argues that the Rabshakeh is effectively offering a "new covenant to supersede that one already in force between Yahweh and Israel."[11]

We here emphasize Hezekiah's choice in terms of competing options, highlighted by the strategic use of the messenger formula. As we mentioned in chapter three, this is the scenario that Ahab faced at the siege of Samaria. Both Ahab and Hezekiah had to yield either to the messenger of the foreign king or to the messenger of Yahweh.

This connection is further bolstered by the strategic use of ḥērem. In the book of Kings, there are only three occurrences of *ḥrm (1 Kgs 9:21; 20:42; 2 Kgs 19:11), and two of them appear in the contexts that we are discussing here. So, while it is clear that the book of Kings does not intend to fully develop a theology of *ḥrm (e.g., the book

<hr>

8. Rudman, "Rabshakeh," 100–110.
9. Rudman, "Rabshakeh," 101.
10. Rudman, "Rabshakeh," 103.
11. Rudman, "Rabshakeh," 108.

TABLE 8: Comparing the use of the messenger formula in
1 Kings 20 and 2 Kings 18–19

King	Foreigner's Use of Messenger Formula	Prophet's Use of Messenger Formula
Ahab	Messengers of Ben-Hadad (1 Kgs 20:5)	Anonymous prophet (1 Kgs 20:13–14, 28)
Hezekiah	Rabshakeh (2 Kgs 18:19) (2 Kgs 18:29, 31 addressed to people)	Isaiah (2 Kgs 19:20) (2 Kgs 19:6 through the envoys of Eliakim, Shebna, and priests)

of Joshua), its double occurence appears strategically located within similar contexts, where foreigners invoke the messenger formula to press the king to make a decision. We therefore perceive a literary connection forged by formal and lexical connections.

We also discussed that the semantics of *ḥērem* relating to its usage in 1 Kings 20 were difficult to clarify, where each context needs to be considered on a case-by-case basis. As such, 2 Kings 19:11 may provide some intriguing possibilities. Amid his monologue, the Rabshakeh states: "Now you have heard about the things which the kings of Assyria did to all the lands, *ḥērem*-ing them. But you will be saved?" This is a rhetorical question that forces Hezekiah to grapple with the legitimacy of his conviction that Judah will somehow escape the same fate that faced all the nations who had stood against the Assyrian Empire. And if one accepts the basic premise of Walton and Walton—that **ḥrm* is not inherently militaristic—in conjunction with our assertion that the semantics of the term must be considered on a case-by-case basis, one may detect how the Rabshakeh's usage suggests a nuance of surrender and vassalship. His question would then essentially communicate: "Now you have heard about the things which the kings of Assyria did to all the lands, killing them if they defied us, removing any sense of governmental autonomy, and imposing our vassalship on them. But you will be saved?"

With this sense, the connection between the opposing responses in the Hezekiah and Ahab contexts is further intensified. Hezekiah refused to accept the Neo-Assyrian ḥērem (vassalship) and trust their provision. Rather, he stood firm in the face of their impending ḥērem and trusted in Yahweh's provision. Conversely, Ahab chose to defy Yahweh's proposed ḥērem set upon his occasional ally, Ben-Hadad of Aram Damascus. Unlike Hezekiah, Ahab opted to disobey Yahweh's terms of engagement for his own political maneuvering. Thus, the major concern in this literary nexus was the obedience of the king, often mediated through prophetic figures, in times of political decision-making. In Yahweh's eyes, it was not about any political dance, but rather obedience and trust, period.

Consequently, it seems that the events of 701 BC could have crystallized the lessons of the Omride *modus operandi* so clearly that the writer connected Hezekiah's trust in Yahweh and his defiance of Sennacherib to the Omride tendency to reject obedience for the sake of political gain. This connection was forged by formal literary means using the messenger formula and was bolstered by a strategic lexeme that communicated issues of political allegiance and vassalship. It seeks to answer two questions. Who is the greater suzerain? What should frame the political and social choices of the community? For Ahab and the Omrides, the answer was found in political expedience and socio-economic opportunity. Although those choices almost brought the Davidic line to an end, for Hezekiah saw this political posturing in action with his father Ahaz, Hezekiah instead chose a policy framed by obedience and allegiance to Yahweh, no matter the cost.

It is possible, therefore, to see this Omride criticism as an element within a larger historiographic program designed to, among other things, celebrate the reign of Hezekiah as the great Judean king who trusted in Yahweh, especially as he defied the Neo-Assyrian army. Although the historical realities of his defiance left Judah devastated, which was an issue that needed a response, by presenting this defiance in terms of absolute obedience and trust in Yahweh—particularly as the antithesis to the villainized Omride dynasty—Hezekiah is to be celebrated.[12]

In the end, we hope this work proves to be useful in the study of biblical historiography and historical reconstruction. Even if one does not accept all our conclusions, it remains clear that biblical history writing and reconstruction are sophisticated endeavors. Understanding all the nuances and details is not possible with superficial readings unaware of ancient literary canons or with a flat consideration of historical sources. Moreover, it remains clear that a proper understanding of biblical history *needs* historical reconstruction, which naturally involves attestations outside the biblical record. They are all part of the same nexus, and they should be mutually influential. It is only by engaging the biblical record in conjunction with its larger environment that the reader is able to fully understand the message of Scripture. Only by consulting the larger environment is the reader able to more precisely understand the message of the biblical writers as they reflected upon the historical experiences of ancient Israel and Judah. Only then is the reader able to appreciate more deeply that the Bible's historical witness is worthy of our trust.

---

12. Schreiner proposes that the account of Sennacherib's siege of Jerusalem functions as a literary anchor in a lengthy historiographic program that not only celebrates Hezekiah in the wake of Sennacherib's devastating siege but also connects said event to the Sea of Reeds event in Exod 14 (David B. Schreiner, "The Annihilation of the Egyptian and Neo-Assyrian Armies: A Proposal of Inner-biblical Typology and Some Literary Critical Implications," *ZAW* 130.4 [2018]: 529–44). In addition, Song-Mi Suzie Park argues that 2 Kings 18–19 ultimately correlates "Pharaoh, the arrogant foreign leader of the Exodus narrative, with Sennacherib, the arrogant foreigner leader in 701" (Park, "Egypt or God? Who Saved Judah from the Assyrian Attack in 701 BCE?," in *Jerusalem's Survival, Sennacherib's Departure, and the Kushite Role in 701 BCE*, ed. Alice Ogden Bellis, Perspectives on Hebrew Scripture and Its Contexts 32 [Piscataway, NJ: Gorgias Press, 2020], 74). While Park's analysis assumes traditional source-critical divisions of 2 Kings 18–19, it nevertheless supports a growing sentiment that 2 Kings 18–19 is constructed not only with a larger historical perspective in view but specifically with an eye toward the exodus. Of course, a context of a Hezekian historical endeavor may not be the only context for which the results may have been originally found. Nevertheless, it is a context that we find particularly reasonable and appealing.

BIBLIOGRAPHY

Albright, William F. "Bronze Age Mounds of Northern Palestine and the Hauran: The Spring Trip of the School in Jerusalem." *Bulletin of the American Schools of Oriental Research* 19 (1925): 5–19.

———. "The Chronology of the Divided Monarchy." *Bulletin of the American Schools of Oriental Research* 100 (1945): 16–22.

———. "One Aphek or Four?" *Journal of the Palestine Oriental Society* 2 (1922): 184–89.

Arnold, Bill T., and John H. Choi. *A Guide to Biblical Hebrew Syntax.* 2nd ed. Cambridge: Cambridge University Press, 2018.

Athas, George. *The Tel Dan Inscription: A Reappraisal and a New Introduction.* The Library of the Hebrew Bible/Old Testament 360. New York: T&T Clark, 2006.

Barr, James. *Comparative Philology and the Text of the Old Testament.* Oxford: Clarendon Press, 1968.

Barrick, W. Boyd. "Another Shaking of Jehoshaphat's Family Tree: Jehoram and Ahaziah Once Again." *Vetus Testamentum* 51.1 (2001): 9–25.

Becking, Bob. "Did Jehu Write the Tel Dan Inscription?" *Scandinavian Journal of the Old Testament* 13 (1999): 187–201.

Bekins, Peter. *Inscriptions from the World of the Bible: A Reader and Introduction to Old Northwest Semitic.* Peabody, MA: Hendrickson Academic, 2020.

Biran, Avraham, and Joseph Naveh. "An Aramaic Stele Fragment from Tel Dan." *Israel Exploration Journal* 43.2–3 (1993): 81–98.

———. "The Tel Dan Inscription: A New Fragment." *Israel Exploration Journal* 45.1 (1995): 1–18.

Bodner, Keith. *The Theology of the Book of Kings*. Old Testament Theology. Cambridge: Cambridge University Press, 2019.

Borowski, Obed. *Daily Life in Biblical Times*. Archaeology and Biblical Studies 5. Atlanta: SBL Press, 2003.

Campbell, Edward F., Jr. "Paul W. Lapp: In Memorium." *The Biblical Archaeologist* 33.2 (1970): 60–62.

Cline, Eric H. *1177 B.C.: The Year Civilization Collapsed*. Turning Points in Ancient History 2. Princeton: Princeton University Press, 2015.

Cogan, Mordechai. *I Kings: A New Translation with Introduction and Commentary*. Anchor Bible 10. New Haven: Yale University Press, 2001.

Cogan, Mordechai, and Hayim Tadmor. "Gyges and Ashurbanipal: A Study in Literary Transmission." *Orientalia* 46.1 (1977): 65–85.

———. *II Kings: A New Translation with Introduction and Commentary*. Anchor Bible 11. New Haven: Yale University Press, 1988.

Cook, John A. "The Semantics of Verbal Pragmatics: Clarifying the Roles of Wayyiqtol and Weqatal in Biblical Hebrew Prose." *Journal of Semitic Studies* 49.2 (2004): 247–73.

Christensen, Duane L. *Deuteronomy 21:10–34:12*. Word Biblical Commentary 6B. Dallas: Word, 2002.

Craigie, Peter C. *The Book of Deuteronomy*. The New International Commentary on the Old Testament. Grand Rapids: Eerdmans, 1976.

———. *Ugarit and the Old Testament*. Grand Rapids: Eerdmans, 1982.

Cundall, Arthur. *Judges and Ruth: An Introduction and Commentary*. Tyndale Old Testament Commentary 7. Downers Grove, IL: InterVarsity Press, 1968.

Dafni, Evangelia G. "רוח שקר und falsche Prophetie in I Reg 22." *Zeitschrift für die alttestamentliche Wissenschaft* 112 (2000): 365–85.

Dallaire, Hélène. *The Syntax of Volitives in Biblical Hebrew and Amarna Canaanite Prose*. Linguistic Studies in Ancient West Semitic 9. Winona Lake, IN: Eisenbrauns, 2014.

Davies, Philip R. *In Search of "Ancient Israel."* Journal for the Study of the Old Testament Supplements 148. Sheffield: JSOT Press, 1992.

Davies, Philip R., and John Rogerson. *The Old Testament World*. 2nd ed. Louisville: Westminster John Knox, 2005.

DeVries, Simon J. *1 Kings*. Word Biblical Commentary 12. 2nd ed. Dallas: Word, 2003.

———. *Prophet against Prophet*. Grand Rapids: Eerdmans, 1978.

Driver, G. R. "Studies in the Vocabulary of the Old Testament II." *Journal of Theological Studies* 32.127 (1931): 250–57.

Duke, Ronald K. "Chronicles, Book of." Pages 161–81 in *Dictionary of the Old Testament: Historical Books*. Edited by Bill T. Arnold and H. G. M. Williamson. Downers Grove, IL: InterVarsity, 2005.

Elayi, Josette. *Sargon II: King of Assyria*. Atlanta: SBL Press, 2017.

Etz, Donald V. "The Genealogical Relationships of Jehoram and Ahaziah and Ahaz and Hezekiah, Kings of Judah." *Journal for the Study of the Old Testament* 71 (1996): 39–53.

Fensham, F. Charles. *The Books of Ezra and Nehemiah*. New International Critical Commentary of the Old Testament. Grand Rapids: Eerdmans, 1983.

Finkelstein, Israel, Oded Lipschits, and Omer Sergi. "Tell er-Rumeith in Northern Jordan: Some Archaeological and Historical Observations." *Semitica* 55 (2013): 7–23.

Fishbane, Michael. *Biblical Interpretation in Ancient Israel*. 1988.
Reprint, Oxford: Clarendon Press, 2004.

Frolov, Serge. *The Turn of the Cycle: 1 Samuel 1–8 in Synchronic and Diachronic Perspectives*. Beihefte zur Zeitschrift für alttestamentliche Wissenschaft 342. Berlin: Walter de Gruyter, 2004.

Garr, W. Randall. *Dialect Geography of Syria-Palestine: 1000–586 B.C.E.* Philadelphia: University of Pennsylvania Press, 1985. Repr., Winona Lake, IN: Eisenbrauns, 2004.

Gass, Erasmus. "Topographical Considerations and Redaction Criticism in 2 Kings 3." *Journal of Biblical Literature* 128.1 (2009): 65–84.

Glueck, Nelson. "Ramoth Gilead." *Bulletin of the American Schools of Oriental Research* 92 (1943): 10–16.

Gmirkin, Russel. "Tool Slippage and the Tel Dan Inscription." *Scandinavian Journal of the Old Testament* 16 (2002): 293–302.

Görg, M. "Aram und Israel." *Vetus Testamentum* 26.4 (1976): 499–500.

Grabbe, Lester. "Reflections on the Discussion." Pages 331–40 in *Ahab Agonistes: The Rise and Fall of the Omri Dynasty*. Edited by Lester L. Grabbe. London: T&T Clark, 2007.

Grayson, A. Kirk. *Assyrian and Babylonian Chronicles*. Winona Lake, IN: Eisenbrauns, 2000.

———. *Assyrian Rulers of the Early First Millennium BC I (1114–859 BC)*. Royal Inscriptions of Mesopotamia, Assyrian Periods 2. Toronto: University of Toronto Press, 1991.

———. *Assyrian Rulers of the Early First Millennium BC II (858–745 BC)*. Royal Inscriptions of Mesopotamia, Assyrian Periods 3. Toronto: University of Toronto Press, 1996.

Greenwood, Kyle R. "Assyrian King List." Pages 368–72 in *The Ancient Near East: Historical Sources in Translation*. Edited by Mark W. Chavalas. Oxford: Blackwell, 2006.

————. "Late Tenth- and Ninth-Century Issues: Ahab Underplayed? Jehoshaphat Overplayed?" Pages 286–318 in *Ancient Israel's History: An Introduction to Issues and Sources*. Edited by Bill T. Arnold and Richard Hess. Grand Rapids: Baker Academic, 2014.

Grossman, Jonathan. *Esther: The Outer Narrative and the Hidden Reading*. Siphrut 6. Winona Lake, IN: Eisenbrauns, 2011.

Hagelia, Hallvard. *The Dan Debate: The Tel Dan Inscription in Recent Research*. Recent Research in Biblical Studies 4. Sheffield: Sheffield Phoenix Press, 2009.

Halpern, Baruch. *David's Secret Demons: Messiah, Murderer, Traitor, King*. Grand Rapids: Eerdmans, 2001.

————. *The First Historians: The Hebrew Bible and History*. University Park, PA: University of Pennsylvania Press, 1996.

Halton, Charles. "How Big Was Nineveh? Literal versus Figurative Interpretation of City Size." *Bulletin of Biblical Research* 18.2 (2008): 193–207.

Hamilton, Victor P. *Exodus: An Exegetical Commentary*. Grand Rapids: Baker Academic, 2011.

Harrison, Roland K., and Edwin M. Yamauchi. "Animal Husbandry." Pages 53–59 in vol. 1 of the *Dictionary of Daily Life in Biblical and Post-biblical Antiquity*. Edited by Edwin M. Yamauchi and Marvin R. Wilson. 4 vols. Peabody, MA: Hendrickson, 2014.

Hasegawa, Shuichi. "Looking for Aphek in 1 Kings 20." *Vetus Testamentum* 62 (2012): 501–14.

Heimpel, Wolfgang. *Letters to the King of Mari: A New Translation, with Historical Introduction, Notes, and Commentary*. Mesopotamian Civilizations 12. Winona Lake, IN: Eisenbrauns, 2003.

Hess, Richard. Review of *Letters to the King of Mari: A New Translation, with Historical Introduction, Notes, and Commentary*, by Wolfgang Heimpel. *Denver Journal* 8 (2005): n.p.

Holland, Drew S. "An Alternative Approach to the Dilemma of
    2 Kgs 3:27." *Asbury Journal of Inductive Biblical Studies* 7.2
    (2020): 7–31.

Horn, Siegfried H. "Why the Moabite Stone was Blown to Pieces."
    Biblical Archaeology Review 12.3 (1986): 30–37.

Jepsen, A. "Israel und Damascus." *Archiv für Orientforschung* 14
    (1942): 154–59.

Kelle, Brad E., and Brent A. Strawn. "History of Israel 5: Assyrian
    Period." Pages 458–78 in *Dictionary of the Old Testament:
    Historical Books*. Edited by Bill T. Arnold and H. G. M.
    Williamson. Downers Grove, IL: IVP Academic, 2005.

King, Philip J., and Lawrence E. Stager. *Life in Biblical Israel*.
    Library of Ancient Israel. Louisville: Westminster John
    Knox, 2001.

Kottsieper, Ingo. "The Tel Dan Inscription (KAI 310) and the
    Political Relations Between Aram-Damascus and Israel in
    the First Half of the First Millennium BCE." Pages 104–34 in
    Ahab Agonistes: The Rise and Fall of the Omri Dynasty. Edited
    by Lester Grabbe. New York: T&T Clark, 2007.

Knapp, Andrew. "The Conflict between Adonijah and Solomon
    in Light of Succession Practices Near and Far." *Journal of
    Hebrew Scriptures* 20, article 2 (2020): 1–26. DOI: 10.5508/
    jhs29557.

———. *Royal Apologetic in the Ancient Near East*. Writings from
    the Ancient World Supplement Series 4. Atlanta: SBL Press,
    2015.

Knauf, Ernst Axel. "The Mists of Ramthalon: How Ramoth-Gilead
    Disappeared from the Archaeological Record." *Biblische
    Notizen* 110 (2001): 33–36.

Knauf, Ernst Axel, D. de Pury, and Thomas Römer. "*Baytdawid
    ou *Baytdod? Une relecture de la nouvelle inscription de Tel
    Dan." *Biblische Notizen* 72 (1994): 60–69.

Kochavi, Moshe, Timothy Renner, Ira Spar, and Esther Yadin. "Rediscovered: The Land of Geshur." *Biblical Archaeology Review* 18 (1992): 30–44.

Kuhrt, Amelié. *The Ancient Near East, c. 3000–330 BC.* 2 vols. London: Routledge, 1997.

Lamb, David T. *Righteous Jehu and His Evil Heirs: The Deuteronomist's Negative Perspective on Dynastic Succession.* Oxford: Oxford University Press, 2008.

Lapp, Nancy L. "Rumeith, Tell er-." Pages 444–45 in vol. 4 of the *Oxford Encyclopedia of Archaeology in the Near East.* Edited by Eric M. Meyers. 5 vols. Oxford: Oxford University Press, 1997.

Lapp, Nancy and Paul Lapp, and Dikran Hadidian, eds. *The Tale of the Tell: Archaeological Studies by Paul W. Lapp.* Eugene, OR: Pickwick, 1975.

Lapp, Paul W. "Tell er-Rumeith." *Revue biblique* 70 (1963): 406–11.

———. "Tell er-Rumeith." *Revue biblique* 75 (1968): 98–105.

Lemaire, André. "The Tel Dan Stele as a Piece of Royal Historiography." *Journal for the Study of the Old Testament* 81 (1998): 3–14.

Lemche, Niels Peter. *Ancient Israel: A New History of Israelite History.* Biblical Seminar 5. Sheffield: JSOT Press, 1988.

Lemche, Niels Peter and Thomas L. Thompson, "Did Biran Kill David? The Bible in Light of Archaeology." *Journal for the Study of the Old Testament* 64 (1994): 3–22.

Leucther, Mark A., and David T. Lamb. *The Historical Writings: Introducing Israel's Historical Literature.* Minneapolis: Fortress, 2016.

Levinson, Bernard M. "The Hermeneutics of Innovation: The Impact of Centralization upon the Structure, Sequence, and Reformulation of Legal Material in Deuteronomy." PhD diss., Brandeis University, 1991.

Lipinski, Edward. *The Arameans: Their Ancient History, Culture, Religion.* Orientalia lovaniensia analecta 100. Leuven: Peeters, 2000.

Liverani, Mario. *Assyria: The Imperial Mission*. Translated by
    Andrea Trameri and Jonathan Valk. Winona Lake, IN:
    Eisenbrauns, 2017.

Lovell, Nathan. *The Books of Kings and Exilic Identity: 1 and 2 Kings
    as a Work of Political Historiography*. The Library of Hebrew
    Bible/Old Testament Studies 708. New York: T & T Clark,
    2021.

Maier, Walter A., III. *1 Kings 12–22*. Concordia Commentary. Saint
    Louis: Concordia Publishing House, 2019.

Malamat, Abraham. "Prophecy at Mari." Pages 50–73 in *The Place
    Is Too Small for Us: The Israelite Prophets in Recent Scholarship*.
    Edited by Robert P. Gordon. Sources for Biblical and
    Theological Study 5. Winona Lake, IN: Eisenbrauns, 1995.

Mattingly, Gerald. "Kir-Hareseth." Page 84 in vol. 4 of *The Anchor
    Bible Dictionary*. 6 vols. Edited by David Noel Freedman.
    New York: Doubleday, 1992.

Mazar, Benjamin. "The Aramean Empire and Its Relations with
    Israel." *The Biblical Archaeologist* 25 (1962): 98–120.

Melville, Sarah C. "Sargon II." Pages 332–42 in *The Ancient Near
    East: Historical Sources in Translation*. Edited by Mark W.
    Chavalas. Oxford: Blackwell, 2006.

McConville, J. G. *Deuteronomy*. Apollos Old Testament
    Commentary 5. Downers Grove, IL: InterVarsity Press,
    2002.

McKenzie, Steven L. *The Trouble with Kings: The Composition
    of the Book of Kings in the Deuteronomistic History*. Vetus
    Testamentum Supplements 42. Leiden: Brill, 1991.

Miller, J. Maxwell. "The Elisha Cycle and the Accounts of the
    Omride Wars." *Journal of Biblical Literature* 85 (1966):
    441–54.

———. "The Fall of the House of Ahab." *Vetus Testamentum* 17.3
    (1967): 307–24.

Miller, J. Maxwell, and John H. Hayes. *A History of Ancient Israel
    and Judah*. 2nd ed. Louisville: Westminster John Knox, 2006.

Monroe, Lauren A. S. "Israelite, Moabite and Sabaean War-
ḥērem Traditions and the Forging of National Identity:
Reconsidering the Sabaean Text RES 3945 in Light of
Biblical and Moabite Evidence." *Vetus Testamentum* 57
(2007): 318–41.

Na'aman, Nadav. "Prophetic Stories as Sources for the Histories of
Jehoshaphat and the Omrides." *Biblica* 78 (1997): 153–73.

———. "Three Notes on the Aramaic Inscription from Tel Dan."
Israel Exploration Journal 50 (2000): 92–104.

North, Robert. "Ap(h)eq(a) and Azeqa." *Biblica* 41.1 (1960): 41–63.

Nuccetelli, S. "Reference and Ethnic Groups." *Inquiry* 14 (2004):
1–17.

Olyan, Saul. "Hăšālôm: Some Literary Considerations of 2 Kings 9."
Catholic Biblical Quarterly 46.4 (1984): 652–68.

Pantiz-Cohen, Naava, and Robert A. Mullins. "Aram-Maacah?
Arameans and Israelites on the Border: Excavations at Tell
Abil el-Qamah (Abel-beth-maacah) in Northern Israel."
Pages 139–68 in *In Search for Aram and Israel: Politics, Culture,
and Identity.* Edited by Omer Sergi, Manfred Oeming, and
Izaak J. de Hulster. Tübingen: Mohr Seibeck, 2016.

Park, Song-Mi Suzie. "Egypt or God? Who Saved Judah from the
Assyrian Attack in 701 BCE?" Pages 55–74 in *Jerusalem's
Survival, Sennacherib's Departure, and the Kushite Role in 701
BCE.* Edited by Alice Ogden Bellis. Perspectives on Hebrew
Scripture and Its Contexts 32. Piscataway, NJ: Gorgias Press,
2020.

Pitard, Wayne T. *Ancient Damascus: A Historical Study of the Syrian
City-State from Earliest Times until Its Fall to the Assyrians in
732 B.C.E.* Winona Lake, IN: Eisenbrauns, 1987.

———. "Paddan-Aram." Pages 55 in vol. 5 of *The Anchor Bible
Dictionary.* 6 vols. Edited by David Noel Freedman. New
York: Doubleday, 1992.

Provan, Iain, V. Philips Long, and Tremper Longman III. *A Biblical
History of Israel.* Louisville: Westminster John Knox, 2003.

Quine, Cat. "Victory as Defeat: Narrative Subversion of Omride Strength in 1 Kings 20." *Journal of Theological Studies* (2021): 1–14. DOI: 10.1093/jts/flab061.

Rainey, Anson, and R. Steven Notley. *The Sacred Bridge: Carta's Atlas of the Biblical World.* Jerusalem: Carta, 2006.

Rasmussen, Carl G. *Zondervan Atlas of the Bible.* Rev. ed. Grand Rapids: Zondervan, 2010.

Redford, Donald. *Egypt, Canaan, and Israel in Ancient Times.* Princeton: Princeton University Press, 1992.

Richelle, Matthieu. "Les conquetes de Hazael selon la recension lucianique en 4 Regnes 13,22." *Biblische Notizen* 146 (2010): 19–25.

Rowton, M. B. "Tuppu and the Date of Hammurabi." *Journal of Near Eastern Studies* 10.3 (1951): 184–204.

Rudman, Dominic. "Is the Rabshakeh also among the Prophets? A Rhetorical Study of 2 Kings XVIII17–35." *Vetus Testamentum* 50.1 (2000): 100–110.

Sader, Hélène. *The History and Archaeology of Phoenicia.* Archaeology and Biblical Studies 25. Atlanta: SBL Press, 2019.

Schmitt, Hans Christoph. *Elisa: Traditionsgeschichtliche Untersuchungen zur vorklassichen nordisraelitischen Prophetie.* Gütersloh: Gütersloher Verlagshaus, 1972.

Schniedewind, William M. "Tel Dan Stela: New Light on Aramaic and Jehu's Revolt." *Bulletin of the American Schools of Oriental Research* 302 (1996): 75–90.

Schreiner, David B. "The Annihilation of the Egyptian and Neo-Assyrian Armies: A Proposal of Inner-biblical Exegesis and Some Literary Critical Implications." *Zeitschrift für die alttestamentliche Wissenschaft* 130.4 (2018): 529–44.

———. "Breaking the Siege: Examining the נַעֲרֵי שָׂרֵי הַמְּדִינוֹת in 1 Kgs 20." *The Asbury Journal* 77.2 (2022): 378–99.

———. "'Now Rehoboam, Son of Solomon, Reigned in Judah': Considering the Structural Divisions of Kings and the

Significance of 1 Kgs 14:21." *Asbury Journal of Inductive Biblical Studies* 7.1 (2020): 7–33.

———. "Omride Dynasty." In *The Lexham Bible Dictionary*. Edited by John D. Barry. Bellingham, WA: Lexham Press, 2016.

———. *Pondering the Spade: Discussing Important Convergences between Archaeology and Old Testament Studies*. Eugene, OR: Wipf and Stock, 2019.

Schreiner, David B., and Kyle R. Greenwood. "An Army Like Goats: A Semantic and Zoological Reconsideration of 1 Kings 20:27." *Vetus Testamentum* (published online ahead of print 2022). DOI: 10.1163/15685330-bja10094.

Sergi, Omer. "The Battle of Ramoth-gilead and the Rise of the Aramean Hegemony in the Southern Levant during the Second Half of the 9th Century BCE." Pages 81–97 in *Wandering Arameans: Arameans Outside Syria; Textual and Archaeological Perspectives*. Edited by Angelika Berlejung, Aren M. Maeir, and Andreas Schüle. Weisbaden: Harrassowitz Verlag, 2017.

Shanks, Hershel, ed. "Biblical Minimalists Meet Their Challengers Face to Face." *Biblical Archaeological Review* 23.4 (1997): 26–42, 66.

Sprinkle, Joe M. "2 Kings 3: History of Historical Fiction?" *Bulletin of Biblical Research* 9 (1999): 247–70.

Steiner, Richard C. "The 'Aramean' of Deuteronomy 26:5: Peshat and Derash." Pages in 127–38 *Telliah le-Moshe: Biblical and Judaic Studies in Honor of Moshe Greenberg*. Edited by M. Cogan, B. L. Eichler, and J. H. Tigay. Winona Lake, IN: Eisenbrauns, 1997.

Stern, Philip. *The Biblical Herem: A Window into Israel's Religious Experience*. Brown Judaic Studies. Atlanta: Scholars Press, 2020.

———. "Of Kings and Moabites: History and Theology in 2 Kings 3 and the Mesha Inscription." *Hebrew Union College Annual* 64 (1993): 1–14.

Stone, Lawson G. "Early Israel and Its Appearance in Canaan."
Pages 127–64 in *Ancient Israel's History: An Introduction to
Issues and Sources*. Edited by Bill T. Arnold and Richard S.
Hess. Grand Rapids: Baker Academic, 2014.

———. "On Historical Authenticity, Historical Criticism, and
Biblical Authority: Reflections on the Case of the Book of
Joshua." *Asbury Theological Journal* 57.2 (2002): 83–96.

———. "Judges." Pages 185–494 in *Joshua, Judges, Ruth*.
Cornerstone Biblical Commentary. Carol Stream, IL:
Tyndale House Publishers, 2012.

Strange, John. "Joram, King of Israel and Judah." *Vetus Testamentum*
25.2 (1975): 191–201.

Suriano, M. J. "The Apology of Hazael: A Literary and Historical
Analysis of the Tel Dan Inscription." *Journal of Near Eastern
Studies* 66 (2007): 163–76.

Svärd, Saana. *Women and Power in Neo-Assyrian Palaces*. Neo-
Assyrian Text Corpus Project. Winona Lake, IN:
Eisenbrauns, 2015.

Sweeney, Marvin A. *I & II Kings*. Old Testament Library.
Louisville: Westminster John Knox, 2007.

Teppo, Saano. "Agency and the Neo-Assyrian Women of the
Palace." *Studia Orientalia* 101 (2007): 381–420.

Thompson, Thomas L. *Early History of the Israelite People*. Studies in
the History of the Ancient Near East 4. Leiden: Brill, 1992.

Tigay, Jeffrey H. "Conflation as a Redactional Technique." Pages
53–96 in *Empirical Models for Biblical Criticism*. Edited by
Jeffrey H. Tigay. Philadelphia: University of Pennsylvania
Press, 1985.

Tolkowsky, S. "Aphek: A Study in Biblical Topography." *Journal of
the Palestine Oriental Society* 2 (1922): 145–58.

Vanderhooft, David S. "Babylonia and the Babylonians." Pages
107–38 in *The World around the Old Testament*. Edited by
Bill T. Arnold and Brent A. Strawn. Grand Rapids: Baker
Academic, 2016.

Verslius, Arie. "Devotion and/or Destruction? The Meaning and Function of חרם in the Old Testament." *Zeitschrift für die Alttestamentliche Wissenschaft* 128.2 (2016): 233–46.

Waltke, Bruce K., and M. O'Connor. *An Introduction to Biblical Hebrew Syntax.* Winona Lake, IN: Eisenbrauns, 1990.

Walton, John H., and J. Harvey Walton. *The Lost World of the Israelite Conquest: Covenant, Retribution, and the Fate of the Canaanites.* Downers Grove, IL: IVP Academic, 2017.

Weinfeld, Moshe. "Ancient Near Eastern Patterns in Prophetic Literature." *Vetus Testamentum* 27 (1977): 178–95.

Wesselius, Jan-Wim. "The First Royal Inscription from Ancient Israel: The Tel Dan Inscription Reconsidered." *Scandinavian Journal of the Old Testament* 13.2 (1999): 163–86.

———. "The Road to Jezreel: Primary History and the Tel Dan Inscription." *Scandinavian Journal of the Old Testament* 15 (2001): 83–103.

White, Marsha. "Naboth's Vineyard and Jehu's Coup: The Legitimation of a Dynastic Extermination." *Vetus Testamentum* 44.1 (1994): 66–76.

Whitelam, Keith W. *The Invention of Ancient Israel: The Silencing of Palestinian History.* London: Routledge, 1996.

Whitley, C. F. "The Deuteronomic Presentation of the House of Omri." *Vetus Testamentum* 2.2 (1952): 137–52.

Wijk-Bos, Johanna W. H. van. *The Land and Its Kings: 1–2 Kings.* Grand Rapids: Eerdmans, 2020.

Wiseman, Donald J. *1 and 2 Kings.* Tyndale Old Testament Commentary 9. 1993. Repr., Downers Grove, IL: IVP Academic, 2008.

———. "The Vassal-Treaties of Esarhaddon." *Iraq* 20.1 (1958): 1–99 and plates.

Wray Beal, Lissa M. *1 & 2 Kings.* Apollos Old Testament Commentary 9. Downers Grove, IL: InterVarsity, 2014.

Würthwein, Ernst. *Die Bücher der Könige: I Kön. 17–II Kön. 25*. Das Alte Testament Deutsch 11.2. Göttingen: Vandenhoeck & Ruprecht, 1984.

———. "Zur Komposition von I Reg 22:1–38." Pages 245–54 in *Das ferne und nahe Wort: Festschrift Leonhard Rost zur Vollendung seines 70 Lebenjahres am 31.11.66 gewidmet*. Edited by F. Maass. Beihefte zur Zeitschrift für alttestamentliche Wissenschaft 105. Berlin: Walter de Gruyter, 1967.

Yamada, Shigeo. "Aram Israel Relations as Reflected in the Aramaic Inscription from Tel Dan." *Ugarit-Forschungen* 27 (1995): 611–25.

Younger, K. Lawson, Jr. *Ancient Conquest Accounts: A Study in Ancient Near Eastern and Biblical History Writing*. Journal for the Study of the Old Testament Supplement Series 98. Sheffield: Sheffield Academic Press, 1990.

———. "Aram and the Arameans." Pages 229–66 in *The World around the Old Testament*. Edited by Bill T. Arnold and Brent A. Strawn. Grand Rapids: Baker Academic, 2019.

———. "'Hazael, son of a Nobody': Some Reflections in Light of Recent Study." Pages 245–270 in *Writing and Ancient Near Eastern Study: Papers in Honour of Alan R. Millard*. Edited by Piotr Bienkowski, Christopher Mee, and Elizabeth Slater. Library of Hebrew Bible/Old Testament Studies 426. New York: T&T Clark, 2005.

———. *A Political History of the Arameans: From Their Origins to the End of Their Polities*. Archaeology and Biblical Studies 13. Atlanta: SBL Press, 2016.

———. "Tiglath-Pileser I and the Initial Conflicts of the Assyrians with the Arameans." Pages 195–228 in *Wandering Arameans: Arameans Outside Syria; Textual and Archaeological Perspectives*. Edited by Angelika Berlejung, Aren M. Maeir, and Andreas Schüle. Wiesbaden: Harrassowitz Verlag, 2017.

IMAGE CREDITS

Figure 1. The Tel Dan Stele. Copyright 2016 Faithlife.

Figure 2. A Relief of Shalmaneser III. Photo by Osama Shukir Muhammed FRCP(Glasg), via Wikimedia Commons, under CC BY 4.0 International.

Figure 3. The Black Obelisk of Shalmaneser III, depicting vassal kings bringing tribute. Photo by Daderot, via Wikimedia Commons, Public Domain.

Figure 4. A stele of the Assyrian queen Sammu-Rāmat. Photo by Osama Shukir Muhammed FRCP(Glasg), via Wikimedia Commons, under CC BY-SA 4.0 International.

Figure 5. The Zakkur Inscription. Copyright 2022 Kyle R. Greenwood.

Figure 6. The Kurkh Monolith Inscription, referencing the Battle of Qarqar and Ahab's role in the Syro-Palestinian coalition. Photo by Osama Shukir Muhammed FRCP(Glasg), via Wikimedia Commons, under CC BY-SA 4.0 International.

Figure 7. *Capra Nubiana* clashing horns, a specific genus that may be behind the imagery of 1 Kings 20:27. Photo by Adam Matan, via Wikimedia Commons, Public Domain.

Figure 8. The Tel Dan Stele, angle view. Copyright 2016 Faithlife.

Figure 9. The topography around Arad—the Israelite coalition would have passed through this territory en route to Moab. Photo by Rob Bye, via Wikimedia Commons, Public Domain.

Figure 10. The Moabite Stone. Copyright 2022 Kyle R. Greenwood.

SUBJECT INDEX

SCRIPTURE INDEX

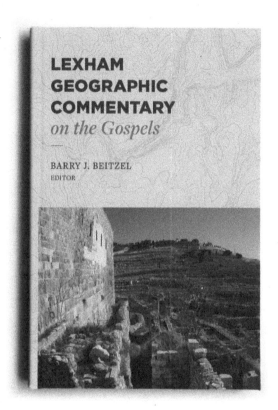